Bushcraft and Gardening for Kids

Master Outdoor Skills and Have Fun with Nature

© **Copyright 2024 - All rights reserved.**

The content contained within this book may not be reproduced, duplicated, or transmitted without direct written permission from the author or the publisher.

Under no circumstances will any blame or legal responsibility be held against the publisher or author for any damages, reparation, or monetary loss due to the information contained within this book, either directly or indirectly.

Legal Notice:

This book is copyright-protected. It is only for personal use. You cannot amend, distribute, sell, use, quote, or paraphrase any part of the content within this book without the consent of the author or publisher.

Disclaimer Notice:

Please note the information contained within this document is for educational and entertainment purposes only. All effort has been executed to present accurate, up-to-date, reliable, and complete information. No warranties of any kind are declared or implied. Readers acknowledge that the author is not engaging in the rendering of legal, financial, medical, or professional advice. The content within this book has been derived from various sources. Please consult a licensed professional before attempting any techniques outlined in this book.

By reading this document, the reader agrees that under no circumstances is the author responsible for any losses, direct or indirect, that are incurred as a result of the use of the information contained within this document, including, but not limited to, errors, omissions, or inaccuracies.

Table of Contents

PART 1: BUSHCRAFT FOR KIDS 1
   INTRODUCTION LETTER TO PARENTS 2
   INTRODUCTION LETTER TO CHILDREN 4
   SECTION 1: WHAT IS BUSHCRAFT? 6
   SECTION 2: BUSHCRAFT GEAR 14
   SECTION 3: CORDAGE AND KNOTS 27
   SECTION 4: BUSHCRAFT SHELTERS 36
   SECTION 5: FIRECRAFT 44
   SECTION 6: WATER AND EDIBLES 53
   SECTION 7: FIRST AID BASICS 62
   SECTION 8: FOOD FINDING SKILLS 71
   SECTION 9: EXTRA BUSHCRAFT SKILLS AND TIPS 80
   THANK YOU MESSAGE 87
PART 2: GARDENING FOR KIDS 89
   INTRODUCTION LETTER TO PARENTS 90
   INTRODUCTION LETTER TO CHILDREN 92
   CHAPTER 1: GARDEN BASICS 94
   CHAPTER 2: TOOLS YOU'LL NEED 101
   CHAPTER 3: FRUITS AND VEGETABLES 108
   CHAPTER 4: HERBS AND FLOWERS 117
   CHAPTER 5: HARVEST TIME 125
   CHAPTER 6: GARDEN FRIENDS AND PESTS 130
   CHAPTER 7: TIPS AND TROUBLESHOOTING 137

CHAPTER 8: FUN GARDEN PROJECTS 145

THANK YOU MESSAGE.. 152

HERE'S ANOTHER BOOK BY DION ROSSER THAT YOU MIGHT LIKE.. 153

REFERENCES 154

IMAGE SOURCES 159

Part 1: Bushcraft for Kids

Mastering the Art of Outdoor Survival and Thriving in the Wilderness

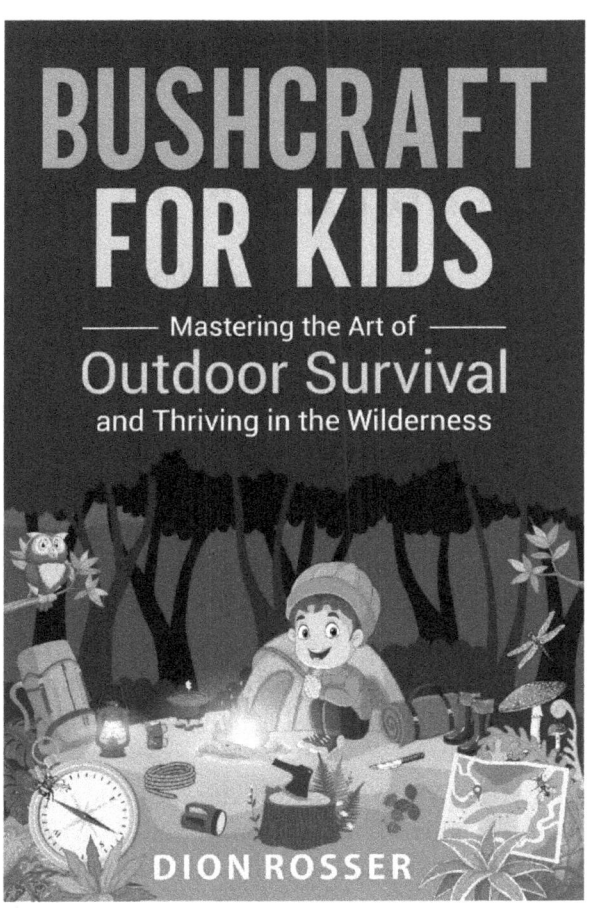

Introduction Letter to Parents

While encouraging children to venture outdoors is essential for their health and well-being, it's natural for parents to be concerned for their safety. It's paramount for children to understand the importance of safety, practical skills to use in the wilderness, and the steps to take in challenging situations. This book is not just about knowing practical skills – it's about using them effectively in the natural world, preparing the child for outdoor exploration.

The purpose of this book extends far beyond teaching outdoor skills. It is a practical guide for your child, nurturing a genuine passion for the great outdoors and creating a connection with nature.

Love for Learning: Through simple explanations, the book aims to ignite a love for learning. Your child will discover the skills of observation, exploration, and discovery to use in the natural world, sparking curiosity and a thirst for knowledge.

Building Confidence: Your child will gain confidence in their abilities by mastering practical skills. This newfound self-assurance can positively impact their overall development and sense of independence.

Environmental Stewardship: The book educates children about the value of nature, the significance of wildlife preservation, and the necessity of keeping the habitat unaffected during their explorations.

Family Bonding: As a parent, you can join your children in these outdoor adventures. The book provides a fantastic opportunity for quality family time, strengthening the parent-child bond and creating cherished memories.

Safety First: Rest assured, the book places utmost importance on safety. Your child will learn essential skills such as first aid, safely foraging food, navigation, and emergency preparedness, ensuring they are well-equipped to handle various outdoor situations responsibly.

The potential risks of nature are unpredictable, which is precisely why extensive safety guidelines and easy-to-understand steps are shared throughout the book. Your child's safety is the utmost priority. This journey will enrich your child's life and create lasting memories and a strong sense of environmental responsibility.

Thank you for entrusting the book with the opportunity to inspire a new generation of responsible and nature-loving explorers.

Introduction Letter to Children

Get ready for a thrilling journey into bushcraft and outdoor survival that gives you life skills that can be used during challenging situations in the wild. The book is more than just words and pages! It takes you to a world where you become the ultimate adventurer while keeping yourself and those around you safe. The journey is not about reading or cramming in information. Instead, it's about doing, experiencing, and embracing the wild while thriving in every situation.

As you read through its pages, you'll discover how to build a shelter, make a fire, find your way in the wilderness, and so much more. These are the skills of true adventurers, skills that empower you to explore the world around you. However, remember that these skills must be used. The more you use them, the more valuable they become. Besides providing an overview of these essential survival skills, you'll be introduced to the basics of foraging food in the wilderness and first aid techniques to face any extreme survival situation with knowledge and confidence.

The wilderness is not just a place to survive. It's also a place to thrive. It's where you'll discover the wonders of nature and the hidden life under every rock. Nature is your teacher, and this book is your guide. You'll learn to venture outdoors, explore the secrets of the woods, climb the peaks, and run along the shorelines. Feel the wind on your face, listen to the songs of the birds, and watch the dance of the trees. Nature is a treasure trove of experiences waiting for you.

Keep this book as your companion because each page will be a stepping stone on your path toward becoming a true explorer. Share your stories with loved ones, see your discoveries, and share your adventures. The wilderness is your playground, and you are its cherished guest. Wishing you an incredible journey.

Section 1: What Is Bushcraft?

Do you love venturing into great outdoor adventures? If yes, you need to learn a set of important wilderness survival skills for your safety and enjoyment to make the most of your outdoor adventure. These survival skills are called bushcraft or survival skills. You need bushcraft skills to live in wild, remote areas or a place that does not have much habitation.

Camping is all about enjoying the natural environment and fun activities. In contrast, *bushcraft* consists of a wide range of practical knowledge and expertise needed to survive and thrive in the wild. Bushcraft includes building a shelter, making a fire, and foraging for food and water. It teaches you how to

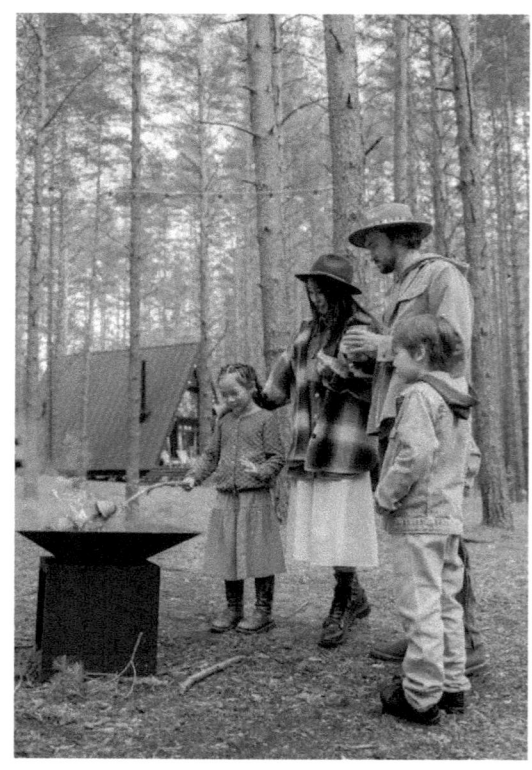

Bushcraft includes building a shelter, making a fire, and foraging for food and water.[1]

rely on yourself, become adaptable, live in the wild with minimal resources, and stay prepared for anything to come. In this section, you will learn all about bushcraft and the outdoor skills that every little adventurer must learn.

Cultural and Historical Importance

Bushcraft or outdoor skills have had great cultural and historical significance throughout various periods and civilizations. People have relied on these skills to survive in nature throughout history. From ancient foraging or hunter-gatherer communities to modern-day civilizations, these skills, including starting a fire, building a shelter, foraging, and the ability to navigate, have always been essential for survival.

These outdoor skills are still quite prominent in many indigenous cultures and are deep-rooted in their way of life. This knowledge is passed down through the generations to preserve traditional techniques and apprehensions. Moreover, this know-how is heavily tied to cultural practices and rituals that reflect the powerful connection between nature and mankind. Bushcraft has also played a huge role in many explorations and historical events. Wilderness skills were extremely important for the survival and success of the early explorers who ventured into new territories and the discoverers who settled into the new lands. These capabilities helped them adapt to new environments, face challenges, and establish developed communities.

Today, bushcraft still holds cultural significance as it fosters resilience, adaptability, self-reliance, and a deep love of nature. It helps you reconnect to your ancestral roots by understanding the elemental skills that equipped your forefathers to survive in the wilderness. Moreover, these skills have become more prominent with the advancement of technology to help you disconnect from the modern world and embrace a simple and sustainable lifestyle. Learning about bushcraft will not only equip you with the ability to survive in the wild, but it will also help you to create a deeper connection with nature, boost self-confidence, and provide a sense of empowerment.

Why Should I Learn Bushcraft?

There are many benefits to learning bushcraft. Learning bushcraft is a rewarding experience that equips you with the skills you need to navigate the challenging situations in the wild and helps you reconnect with your primal instincts and innate capabilities. Here is a list of reasons why you should consider learning bushcraft:

You'll Learn Independence

Bushcraft teaches you the necessary skills to survive. By learning these skills, you will learn how to take care of yourself, fostering a sense of confidence and self-reliance in yourself. Learning basic life-saving skills such as building a fire, constructing a shelter, and getting clean water and food are wonderful forms of self-reliance that will teach you how to survive with minimal resources if you ever find yourself in an unfortunate situation.

It Teaches You Critical Thinking and Problem-Solving Skills

Bushcraft skills help you develop the ability to analyze situations, find solutions, and adapt to new circumstances. You will need creative problem-solving skills and quick thinking to survive in the wilderness. These skills are also important for navigating other aspects of your life, including school projects and personal challenges.

Creates Environmental Awareness

Bushcraft and outdoor skills deeply connect you to nature. As you learn to thrive in natural environments, you will become more environmentally conscious and appreciate the world around you. Using environmentally-friendly techniques will nurture a desire to save the planet.

Makes You More Adaptable and Resourceful

As you know, you will have limited resources in the wild. Children who learn bushcraft skills become more self-reliant and resourceful as they navigate difficult situations using natural resources efficiently. They become more adaptable and believe they can find a way out in all situations, including those in their everyday lives.

Makes You Physically Fit

Bushcraft skills require a lot of physical exertion, which is bound to make you physically stronger. These skills allow you to develop an appreciation for outdoor activities and become more physically active.

You'll Gain Crisis Management Skills

You can save lives in emergencies with bushcraft skills. Crisis management skills such as emergency signaling, navigation, and learning first aid will prepare you for unexpected situations.

Boosts Your Confidence and Resilience

Becoming self-reliant will boost your self-confidence. These essential life-saving skills make you believe you can overcome adversity and challenges. It makes you more resilient, and you begin to understand that you can handle life's uncertainties with composure and persistence.

Opportunity to Educate Others

Once you become a pro at bushcraft, and if you're passionate about it, you can also teach these essential skills to others. Share your knowledge of these practical skills with your friends, family, and other kids in your school or the neighborhood.

Outdoor Recreation

Bushcraft is an excellent way to enhance your amusement experiences. It will make your outdoor experiences, whether camping, backpacking, or hiking, significantly more enjoyable and adventurous.

You'll feel accomplished when you discover you can manage the fire safely, cook meals, and take on responsibilities involved in survival. These survival skills are useful because they make you self-reliant, humble, and nature-loving.

Respect Nature and Leave No Trace Behind

Care for the environment and leave it how you found it. You can enjoy and benefit from nature without disturbing the ecosystem or leaving any traces of your presence. Here are some ways in which you can minimize your impact on the environment:

Minimize Pollution

Be cautious of the waste you generate while in natural environments. Make sure to pack up all your litter and limit the use of disposable items. You must pick up after yourself and carefully dispose of your trash.

Do Not Create New Trails

Use the established trails to prevent soil erosion and habitat disruption. Creating new trails can also cause damage to wildlife habitats and vegetation.

Do Not Disturb the Wildlife

If you come across a wild animal, you may observe them from afar and try not to disturb or feed them. Feeding these wild animals can disrupt their diets and natural behaviors and may lead to unhealthy interactions between animals and humans.

Use Sustainable Transportation

Make sure to use sustainable means of transportation to visit these natural areas. You may use your bike, carpool with your friends, or use public transportation to reduce your carbon footprint.

Save Water

Take special care of your water usage while exploring nature. Being mindful of your water consumption can reduce the danger of water contamination through soap, detergents, or other pollutants.

Educate Yourself

Learning about the wildlife and natural areas you visit will help you understand the fragility of your environment. It can lead you to make better decisions and utilize careful behaviors while you're out there.

Do Not Disturb the Natural and Cultural Artifacts

Leave the natural or cultural artifacts as you found them. This includes plants, rocks, and historical relics. Avoid removing these artifacts and leave them for the next person to enjoy and appreciate.

Inspire Others

You can share your knowledge and inspire others to care for the environment and the natural and cultural artifacts. You must encourage your loved ones to learn and obey the essential principles of the "Leave No Trace" movement.

You must respect nature by utilizing the techniques mentioned above to ensure that you leave minimal environmental impact. It is important to take care of the ecosystem's delicate balance to ensure that future generations also get to appreciate it. Everyone should play their part in protecting the environment.

Bushcraft Activities Deepen Your Connection to the Natural World

Nature is the greatest teacher. Learning bushcraft skills allows you to connect and develop your relationship with nature. It has a healing effect that boosts happiness and physical and emotional well-being. It awakens your sense of peace. Here is how nature has a healing impact on humans:

Enhances Your Observation and Awareness

Your awareness of your surroundings and observational skills are heightened with bushcraft. You will notice subtle environmental cues, such as recognizing edible vegetation, tracking wildlife, and identifying weather changes. Bushcraft will enhance your understanding of the world around you and your importance in it.

Respect for Your Surroundings

Learning bushcraft helps you develop a deeper respect for nature. It empowers you to rely on natural resources to fulfill your needs and develop a sense of responsibility and gratitude for the environment that provides these resources.

Mindfulness and Presence

Bushcraft exercises require one to remain present in the moment. It is important to practice mindfulness to stay safe and thrive in the wilderness.

Connect to Traditional Knowledge

Many bushcraft skills are deep-rooted in the indigenous knowledge passed down through generations. You can strengthen your relationship with the natural world and connect with the wisdom of your ancestors by practicing these skills.

Importance of Safety and Responsible Outdoor Behavior

You must be responsible during your outdoor adventures. Your actions impact yourself, others, and the environment. Here are some ways you can stay safe and enjoy the outdoors.

Injury Prevention and Well-Being

You must adhere to the safety guidelines while learning bushcraft or other outdoor activities, including camping, hiking, and water sports. Behaving responsibly will help you stay secure while having fun. Keep yourself hydrated and wear appropriate clothing and gear to maintain good health.

Environmental Conservation

You must protect the environment at all costs and refrain from littering, vandalism, and engaging in reckless behavior, as it can lead to uncontrolled fires and damage the ecosystems and natural habitats.

Ethical Considerations

Respect people around you and engage in behavior that does not ruin anyone else's experience. Allow other people to connect with nature without any distractions. You must also be mindful of the cultural and historical sites and treat these sites with respect.

Community and Social Responsibility

Prepare for emergencies and make sure you always adhere to the safety protocols. Moreover, try your best to follow the trail etiquette and avoid overcrowding a place.

How to Plan the First Bushcraft Adventure

Do you want to know how to plan your first bushcraft adventure? You must prioritize comfort, safety, and enjoyment. Here are some tips to plan your bushcraft adventure:

Choose a Safe Location

Choose a location that is safe, easily accessible, and has a manageable terrain.

Check the Weather Forecast

Before setting out on an adventure, pack clothing and appropriate gear to deal with unexpected weather conditions. Prepare for rain as well.

Appropriate Gear

You need a sleeping bag, a backpack, and clothing of your size that fits comfortably.

Simple Shelter

Ensure you have a simple and steady shelter that is easy to assemble and protects you from other environmental elements.

Food and Water

Plan your meals and snacks and ensure you have everything you need to make the food you need. Also, make sure you have access to clean water.

Supervision

It is wise to be accompanied by a responsible and experienced adult.

Basic Skills

Learn age-appropriate basic bushcraft skills such as identifying edible plants, setting up campfires, and using navigation tools like compasses.

Fun Activities

Engage in fun activities like scavenger hunts, storytelling, watersports, stargazing, etc., to enhance your outdoor experience.

Comfort Items

Pack your favorite blankie, toy, or pillow to feel better in the wild.

First-Aid Kit

Ensure you have access to a first aid box to deal with injuries or illnesses.[2]

Ensure you have access to a first aid box to deal with injuries or illnesses.

In this section, you learned the basics of bushcraft. Remember that as you learn these essential survival skills, you must take care of yourself and remain prepared for emergencies. You can have the most fun while staying responsible and engaging in safe behaviors while taking care of the environment.

Section 2: Bushcraft Gear

Taking a bushcraft kit with you on an outdoor adventure is essential for several reasons. First, it's a matter of survival and safety. A well-equipped bushcraft kit contains tools and gear crucial to keep you safe and secure in the wilderness. Whether cutting tools for various tasks, fire-starting equipment to provide warmth and cook food, or materials for building a shelter, these items are invaluable in challenging situations.

Furthermore, you become more self-sufficient outdoors, reducing your dependence on external assistance. This level of preparedness is necessary for emergencies, where your kit can mean the difference between comfort and difficulty. Beyond survival, a bushcraft kit allows you to maximize your use of natural resources. With the right tools and knowledge, you can adapt to your surroundings, finding shelter, fire, and sustenance solutions.

Likewise, you can cook hot meals, stay warm, and create a secure sleeping arrangement, which is vital for extended trips. It serves a dual purpose of providing safety and contains tools necessary for outdoor explorations.

In this chapter, you'll learn about bushcraft gear components, including the tools and equipment needed to make your outdoor adventures a breeze.

Shelter and Sleep

Shelters are a makeshift outdoor home to make when you want to stay at a place for further exploration.[3]

Shelters are a makeshift outdoor home to make when you want to stay at a place for further exploration. Sleeping sacks, tents, and tarps are some standard items used for shelter in the wild. They keep you cozy and dry in rainy weather and protect you from wandering bugs or insects that could harm you during sleep.

Types of Shelters: Although shelters come in different shapes and sizes, tents are the most feasible for a family adventure. These are portable homes set up for more than one person to use. Tarps are also popular as these waterproof blankets are compact to carry and can be set up instantly. You also have the option of a bivouac sack, which is a sleeping bag for your body. These snug sleeping sacks are also waterproof and insulated to keep you dry and warm. The type of shelter you pick will depend on the days you'll live outdoors, the number of people going, and the weather conditions.

Setting up Your Shelter: It's not difficult to set up a shelter as long as you know the proper steps to execute.

1. Find an even and clear spot if you're setting up a tent.
2. Lay out the tent and make a footprint for reference.
3. Assemble the tent poles and place them on the footprint you made earlier.

4. Attach the tent body to the pole structure, and it's all done.

While you won't find it hard to set up sleeping sacks or tarps, tents can come in several forms, and their assembly procedure can vary too. If you have trouble setting up the tent, review the instructions from the tent's user manual for better understanding. Just like you assembled the tent, you can disassemble it by reversing the order of instructions. When you've finished your trip, check the tent for damage, clean it, and store it properly so it can be used for your next outdoor adventure.

Sleeping Essentials

Your bushcraft gear should contain sleeping essentials like sleeping bags, mats, and blankets to keep you extra comfy and protected from the weather.'

Besides packing shelter essentials, your bushcraft gear should contain sleeping essentials like sleeping bags, mats, and blankets to keep you extra comfy and protected from the weather. Although there are several sleeping essentials, it's best to pick travel-friendly quilts and blankets and even pack hammocks when exploring the wild in the summer.

Cutting Tools

Knives are your trusty tools for cutting things during your camping adventures. They always come in handy, from making marshmallow sticks to opening canned packages. Likewise, camping axes and saws are excellent for chopping wood and making campfires. However, you must use these tools with extreme caution and under the supervision of a family member to ensure safety. After every outdoor trip, keep your cutting tools clean and sharp, and store them in perfect condition for the next trip.

A bushcraft knife is easy to handle and use for many tasks.[5]

A bushcraft knife is not the regular household knife used to cut fruit in the kitchen; it's made of sturdy blade material and comes in many forms. You can purchase a bushcraft knife according to size preference and handle design. The right knife should fit comfortably in your hand, be durable, and suit your intended tasks, such as cutting, carving, or other outdoor needs.

Fire-Making Gear

These tools are used mainly to create warm campfires, cook food, or even to signal for help if you need assistance during escapades. There are a variety of fire-starting tools and materials to pick from. Here are some common ones you can add to your bushcraft gear.

Firesteel and Flint: In old times, flint and steel were struck together to produce sparks and ignite dry tinder. Nowadays, modern firesteel comes with a steel rod to generate sparks, making fire-starting hassle-free. Firesteel is also much more reliable when used in extreme weather conditions.

Firesteel and flint makes lighting a fire super easy.[6]

Ferrocerium Rods: Ferrocerium rods, often called ferro rods, create hot sparks when scraped with a hard object, like the back of a knife. They're highly durable and work in wet conditions, making them a dependable tool for igniting dry tinder in the wild.

Waterproof Matches and Lighters: Waterproof matches have treated heads that resist water and light even when damp, while lighters produce a flame when ignited. They are excellent backup tools for starting fires during camping or emergencies. However, you must keep lighters dry for reliable use.

Tinder and Fuel: Tinder and fuel are the unique ingredients for your campfire magic. They make the wood catch fire quickly, like adding sticks and paper to burn brightly.

Containers and Hydration

Water Containers: Whether you want electrolyte water on the go or prefer drinking plain water, you'll need containers and water bottles. They ensure you stay hydrated by holding your water so you have enough to drink during outdoor adventures.

Water containers are important to keep you hydrated.[7]

Water Purification Tools: You can add portable water purification gadgets to the bushcraft kit to ensure your drinking water is clean and safe. Water purification tablets, water filters for backpackers, and portable sediment filters can be used for water purification. You can pick a feasible method according to the adventure you are planning. Despite all these methods, you can still go for the old-school method of boiling water before drinking if you're not carrying any water purification gadget or tool.

Navigation and Signaling
Navigation Tools:

Navigation tools are your guides in the wilderness. They include maps and compasses that help you find your way when you're out exploring so you don't get lost.

Navigation tools are your guides in the wilderness.[8]

Signaling and Communication: Signaling and communication tools are your way to send secret messages to your friends or call for help if you need it. They're like your adventure walkie-talkies and signal to get assistance when you're on exciting adventures.

First Aid and Safety

First Aid Kits: First aid kits are your superhero kits for when you get a little hurt. They contain band-aids, medicine, and other things to help you feel better if you have a small injury during outdoor fun. This can include creams for insect bites.

Safety Gear: Safety gear is like your adventure superhero outfit. It includes headlamps to light your way, bear spray to keep animals away, and cool tools to keep you safe and make your outdoor experiences amazing.

Safety gear like a headlamp makes it easier for you to walk around the camp at night.[9]

Backpacks

Choosing the Right Backpack: Selecting the right backpack is like choosing the right-sized backpack for school. It's important because it should comfortably hold all your gear. Consider factors like size, capacity, and features based on the length and type of trip you are going on.

Packing Your Backpack Efficiently: Think of packing your backpack like organizing your school bag. Efficient packing involves placing heavier items closer to your back so that the load is well balanced, using compartments wisely, and keeping essential gear easily accessible. It ensures a comfortable and well-balanced load.

Adjusting and Fitting Your Pack: Adjusting and fitting your backpack is like wearing your school bag with the right straps and adjustments to keep it comfortable. Straps, hip belts, and shoulder straps should be adjusted to your body for a snug and well-distributed load, preventing discomfort during your outdoor journey.

Make sure you get the right backpack that's easy to carry and holds everything you need.[10]

Clothing Essentials

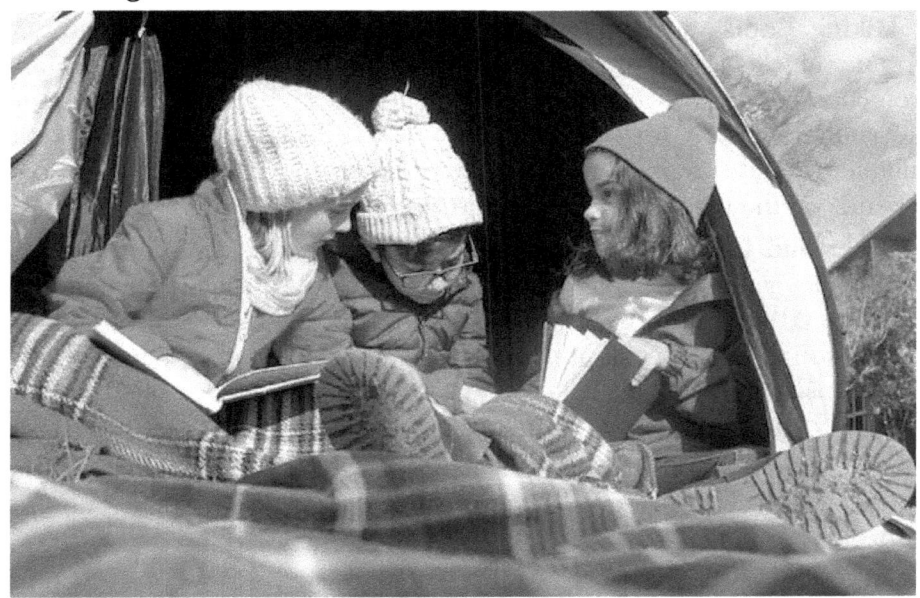

Dress right for the adventure when in the wild.[11]

Dress right for the adventure when in the wild. You have three layers to consider:

Base Layers: These are cozy pajamas for the outdoors. These clothes are closest to your skin, designed to keep you warm and dry by wicking away sweat. They act like insulation in cold weather, trapping heat close to your body. Cotton is a wise choice.

Mid-Layers: Mid-layers are like your regular clothes for the outdoors. They provide insulation to keep you warm but are also breathable, preventing you from getting too sweaty. They are extra layers to stay cozy.

Outer Layers: Consider the outer layers your *superhero cape*. They shield you from the elements, like rain, wind, and snow. These layers keep you dry and protect you from the weather, ensuring you stay comfortable in harsh conditions.

Headwear and Gloves: Headwear and gloves are your secret armor, keeping you warm and protected against the cold. Hats keep your head warm, and gloves guard your hands. They're essential for comfort and prevent frostbite in chilly weather.

Footwear

Hiking Boots vs. Trail Shoes: Hiking boots are the heavy-duty, all-terrain vehicles of footwear. They provide strong ankle support and protection against rough trails and heavy loads. Trail shoes, however, are like sporty sneakers for the outdoors. They're lighter and more flexible, suitable for less demanding hikes and faster movement. Your choice depends on the type of terrain and the weight you'll be carrying.

Socks and Gaiters: Think of socks as your cozy cushioning for your feet, while gaiters are like leg protectors. Good-quality socks provide comfort and help prevent blisters. Conversely, gaiters shield your legs and boots from dirt, rocks, and moisture, especially in rugged or wet conditions.

Foot Care in the Wilderness: Foot care is like looking after your favorite shoes. Maintain healthy feet by managing blisters, keeping your feet dry, and choosing proper footwear for an enjoyable and pain-free outdoor adventure.

Ten Essential Items for Bushcraft Gear

These items are crucial for safety and survival in the outdoors. Each item serves a specific purpose to prepare you for various situations. Here are the ten essentials and their importance.

1. Navigation

Map: A detailed, up-to-date topographic map of the area you'll be exploring.

Compass: A reliable compass for navigation, especially in areas without clear trails or signage.

You need a map and a compass to navigate.[12]

2. Insulation

Extra Clothing: Layers to help you stay warm and dry, including a hat and gloves.

3. Illumination

Headlamp/Flashlight: Provides light in low-light conditions or emergencies.

4. First Aid Supplies

First Aid Kit: Treats injuries and medical emergencies in the field.

A first aid kit will help with emergency situations.[18]

5. Fire Starter

Firesteel, Waterproof Matches, or Lighter: Critical for starting fires in emergencies, for warmth, cooking, and signaling.

6. Repair Tools and Kits

Multi-Tool and Repair Kits: Useful for gear repair and other tasks that may arise during your trip.

7. Nutrition

Extra Food: Non-perishable, high-energy snacks that can sustain you if your trip takes longer than expected.

8. Hydration

Water and Filtration/Purification: You need access to clean drinking water and avoid waterborne illnesses by using water purification methods.

9. Emergency Shelter

Emergency Blanket or Tarp: Provides shelter and protection from the elements in unexpected situations.

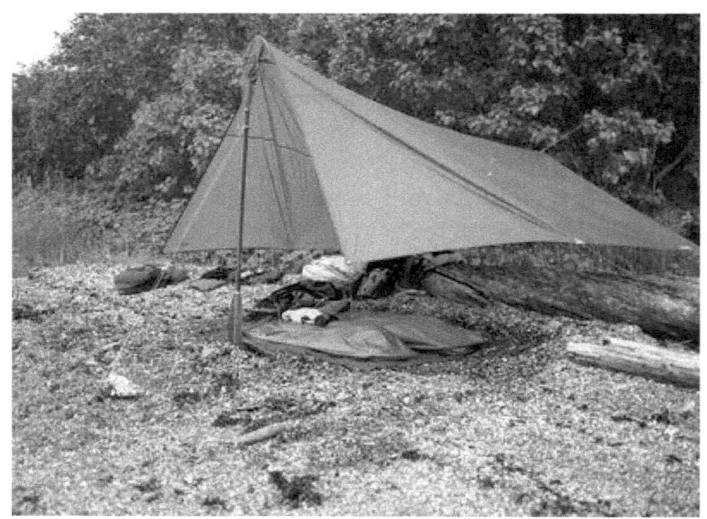
A tarp is useful if it starts raining or if you need to rest.[14]

10. Sun Protection

Sunscreen, Sunglasses, and a Hat: Protect yourself from sunburn and UV exposure, especially in high-altitude or snow-covered environments.

The ten essentials are designed to help you navigate, survive, and stay safe in the wilderness. Remember to customize your gear based on your outdoor adventure's specific conditions and location.

Optional Gear for Comfort and Convenience

If your trip is short and you won't be doing much exploration, consider these items for comfort:

- Camp Chair
- Multi-Tool
- Solar Charger
- Insect Repellent
- Camp Pillow
- Cookware Set
- Camp Stove
- Portable Water Heater
- Camp Shower
- Portable Coffee Maker

Bushcraft Gear for Specific Seasons

As explained earlier, you must consider several factors when preparing your gear. Besides your personal requirements, the biggest influential factors are the weather and terrain. Here are some bushcraft gear samples for different seasons – so you know which items to pack. Please remember that the essential items listed above are already included in the gear but not mentioned here.

Gear List for Woodlands (Spring/Summer)
- Additional clothing that is lightweight and has breathable layers
- Bug repellent
- Folding saw or small hatchet (for wood processing)
- Insect head net

Gear List for Deserts (Fall/Winter)
- Sun-protective clothing and layers for cold nights
- Wide-brimmed hat
- Extra sunscreen and lip balm
- Bandana or shemagh (for protecting your face from sun and dust)

Gear List for Mountains (Winter)

Know the specific challenges and conditions of the environment and season you'll be venturing into.[15]

- Insulated and waterproof layers
- Crampons and ice ax (for snowy or icy conditions)
- Snow goggles
- Avalanche safety gear (if in avalanche-prone areas)
- Snowshoes (for deep snow)

Know the specific challenges and conditions of the environment and season you'll be venturing into. Customize your gear list accordingly and ensure you have the skills and knowledge to use each item effectively in those conditions. Additionally, always inform someone about your trip plans and expected return time when heading to more remote or challenging environments.

Section 3: Cordage and Knots

Think about building a shelter in the woods. You will use many materials like branches and leaves. Now, imagine that you need to catch some fish. You may need a net. If you do not have a backpack, tie up your belongings to carry them easier. While ducking and dodging trees or shrubs, some of your clothing can get ripped, which you will need to repair, especially if you are spending extended periods in the wild. From your shelter to your tools and your traps for animals, cordage is useful for many of your bushcraft needs. Therefore, you must be skilled in using and tying knots in ways that can help with a broad range of issues that come up in nature.

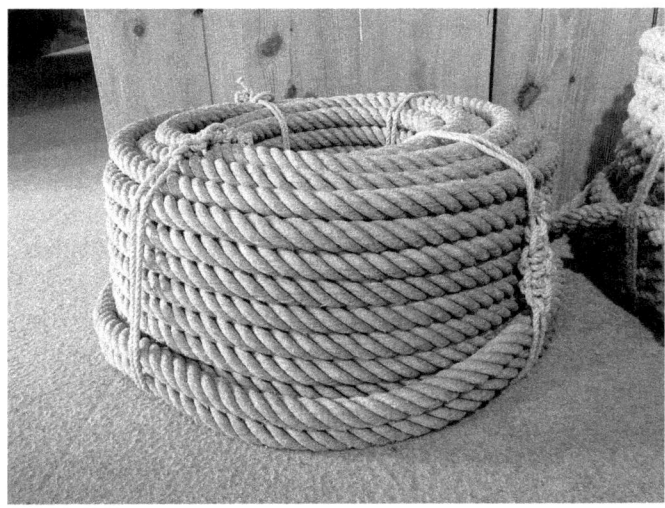

Cordage is a fancy word for rope or string.[16]

Cordage is a fancy word for rope or string. Naming all the uses for cordage in the wild is almost impossible because, with rope, only your imagination limits you. However, it helps to know a few basics when you are starting. Carrying a role of cordage in your pocket can come in handy in multiple situations you would not normally think of. Take a look around your house and see all the places where cord, string, and ropes are used. No survival kit is complete with it. So, what happens if you forget to take rope on a trip into the bush? True survivalists use their surroundings to their advantage. Cordage in the wild is abundant, with both plant and animal sources. Nature gives you everything you need. This section will teach you how to use cordage in different ways and how to identify cordage materials in the wilderness.

Cordage and Its Many Forms

Cordage can take many forms, including natural and synthetic materials. Your cordage can either be neatly packed rope or line you brought on the trip with you or something you crafted from other items you had on you, depending on how innovative and creative you are. Historically, cordage was one of the first significant technological leaps of Stone Age people. The invention of cordage in different forms helped hunter-gatherers travel more easily, hunt with more efficiency, and, later on, construct systems for watering crops and constructing boats for sailing. The use of cordage is only limited by your expertise and your imagination. Therefore, understanding the basics of cordage use could transform the way you think about survival as you constantly discover new ways to use it.

Natural Sources of Cordage Material

The purpose of bushcraft is to know how to survive in the wilderness with limited access to resources. Whether you are forcefully flung into a survival situation or lose your rope on a camping trip, knowing how to make cordage from natural material is a specialized skill that can be life-saving. To the trained eye and skilled hands, nature is a general store. For plant or animal materials to be suitable for cordage, they must meet a few conditions; namely, they must be strong, flexible, and easy to tie. Not every organism in the woods meets this criteria, and the geographical area you are in also has its unique conditions that will affect the cordage you can harness. Therefore, you need a background understanding of a few basic principles. Mastering the bush is all about knowing what to look for and how to craft it into exactly what you need.

Plant Fibers

Many plants can be used for cordage as long as their fibers are strong and flexible. First, you must be sure that a plant or a tree is not toxic when you handle it. This is why any survivalist must educate themselves about the different species of plants in the areas they explore. One of the easiest ways to get cordage from plants is to find a tree with some dry bark that you can easily strip. Underneath the bark, you will find a fibrous cambium layer, the soft, stringy material on the surface of the tree, and the back of the bark. You notice the fibrous cambium makes strings when you rip the dry bark off. You also have the option of stripping wet bark and allowing it to dry in the sun. Be mindful that you can damage trees and kill them, so make sure not to cut too deeply into the trunk. Some leaves are also suitable for cordage. The key is to find long, stringy materials that you can manipulate, bend, and tie.

Animal Sinew

Unlike plant cordage, which can pretty much be used immediately, animal sinew requires some processing. Traditional culture used big game like elk or deer from which to extract sinew. The long tendons in the legs of these giant beasts are the best part to use for cordage.

You will first need to cut the tendons carefully from the legs with a sharp knife. It is best if someone skilled and knowledgeable helps you with this.

Next, you must clean off all the excess meat and fat. Once the sinew is cleaned, you will need to dry it for a few days. Once all the moisture is out of the sinew, pound it with a hammer until it smooths out. This beating increases the strength and flexibility of the sinew. Lastly, you must twist the strands of sinew together and stretch them out to be useful for wilderness applications.

Commercial Cordage Options

Most of the time, you will not be in the bush due to an unfortunate accident or survival event. Therefore, you will be able to carry the cordage of your choice on you. When choosing which types of string or ropes to use, you must consider how adaptable they are in various situations, how heavy they are because you will be carrying them, and how strong and flexible the cord is. The most commonly preferred cordage options for bushcraft are nylon and paracord. Scientists are always developing strong and lightweight materials, so there are always new varieties of outdoor cordage to try at specialized camping stores. Each of these materials has its benefits and disadvantages, so you must figure out what works best for your goals.

Paracord

Paracord is a type of kernmantle rope, meaning it has an interior wrapped in woven fabrics.[17]

Paracord is a type of kernmantle rope, meaning it has an interior wrapped in woven fabrics. Much like nylon, paracord is strong and holds its shape quite well over time. One of the advantages of paracord is that it does not hold moisture like nylon, so it will not develop mold or mildew in moist environments. Paracord is relatively cheap compared to other rope materials with a similar strength. The downside of using paracord rope is that it can become tangled, which is an issue for someone with limited space in a backpack in the wilderness and who is constantly traveling. Furthermore, paracord tends to come in long sections, which could make it even more difficult to store.

Nylon

Nylon rope is the strongest synthetic rope on the market.[18]

Nylon rope is the strongest synthetic rope on the market, and its flexibility makes the rope shock absorbent, meaning that if something was attached to the rope and it fell, it reduces the chances of getting damaged. Nylon returns to its original size after it has been stretched and does not break easily. Plus, its durability and flexibility allow it to be used in many sticky situations that you can run into outdoors. The cons of using nylon rope are that it absorbs a lot of water, which weakens the rope and shrinks the material when wet, so it is probably not great for moist environments like forests.

Fundamental Knots

Having some knowledge of knots you can quickly remember will make you a shining star in the bush. You'd be surprised how often you find yourself having to tie objects together in the wilderness. Your effectiveness in the woods is greatly increased when you know how to use your cordage properly. Freestyling knots can be dangerously ineffective and have disastrous outcomes. Therefore, you must be educated on how to use your rope, string, and any other cordage well.

Square Knot

The square knot is used to tie a rope to an object. In a wilderness scenario, a square knot can tie bundles together, making objects like branches easier to carry. In some cases, square knots are tied around open wounds to stop bleeding. Therefore, this amazing knot can be used in numerous ways.

1. To tie a square knot, begin by passing one end of a rope or string over another.
2. Then, take the same end and pass it underneath the other end of the rope.
3. Repeat the crossing motion you did with the two remaining sections of rope.
4. Pull on both ends to tighten the knot. You can repeat the process, making a few knots on top of one another for more security.

The square knot is used to tie a rope to an object.[19]

This is one of the most basic knots to tie, and many people learned it when they began tying their shoelaces.

Bowline

The bowline knot is used to secure a rope to a standing object like a tree or a pole. In the bush, this knot can tie down a shelter or belongings you do not want to lose.

1. For the first step of tying a bowline, you must create a loop in your cordage.
2. Next, grab the rope's end and pass it underneath the loop before pulling it through the center of the hole you have created.
3. Now, wrap the end of the rope you have passed through the loop around the standing section of the cordage.
4. Then push the rope back through the loop you created and then pull to tighten.

The bowline knot is used to secure a rope to a standing object like a tree or a pole.[20]

Taut-Line Hitch

The taut-line hitch knot is a very useful sliding knot to secure or carry items. The beauty of this knot is that it tightens under a load and can be slid easily for release, making it adaptable for multiple applications.

1. Start by looping a rope around the item, like a bucket handle or a post.
2. Take the rope's end and make another loop around the standing line. The loop should be made working towards the post your rope is around.
3. Now, make another loop around the standing line outside of the loop you had previously made.
4. After tightening the knot, you will be able to make the loop on the end of the rope bigger or smaller by sliding the knot back and forth.

The taut-line hitch knot is a very useful sliding knot to secure or carry items.[21]

Clove Hitch

Clove hitch knots are used to secure a rope to a horizontal pole, stick, or branch. This knot is great for suspending valuables like pots or food out of the reach of various animals in the woods. The knot has also been used for rock climbing and sailing. However, note that a clove hitch knot can come loose when faced with enough tension, so it is best used in combination with other knots.

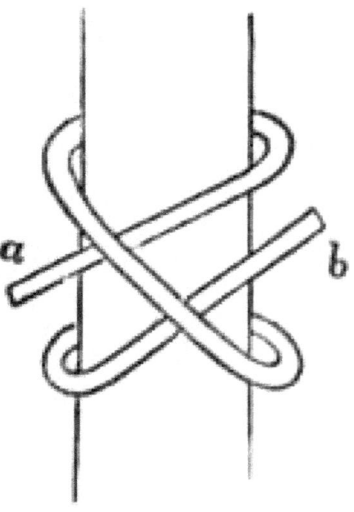

- Wrap your cordage around a horizontal pole or stick to tie a clove hitch.

- Next, cross the end of your rope over the already-wrapped section around the stick.

- Then thread the rope's end under the second loop you made and pull to tighten.

Clove hitch knots are used to secure a rope to a horizontal pole, stick, or branch.[22]

Choosing the Right Knot

The knot you choose will depend on what you are trying to achieve by tying your rope of string. Consider asking whether you need a string knot that can support a lot of weight or an adjustable knot. Other questions you can ask yourself include: will a simple knot be sufficient, or do you need a knot that can be easily loosened? By analyzing your goals and then exploring the knots you have learned, you can match the exact knot you need with the task you want to complete.

Tips, Tricks, and Common Mistakes

Some common mistakes when using cordage are not double-checking your knots and using the wrong kind of rope. Different rope types are unsuited for certain conditions, and some knots are incompatible with some materials. So, ensure you use the right material paired with the right knots while carefully double or even triple-checking your knots to prevent accidents. The biggest tip that can be given regarding cordage is to make sure that it is both durable and flexible so that it can be used for multiple wilderness applications. Ask at a camping supply shop as often their staff are quite knowledgeable on which ropes to use.

Section 4: Bushcraft Shelters

Your most basic needs are food, air, water, clothing, and shelter. If you are ever in a survival situation in the wilderness, shelter is one of the first needs to be taken care of. Constructing an effective shelter should be at the top of your priority list. In some circumstances, you may feel that lighting a fire should be your first priority. However, in some emergencies, you should build a shelter first. Most people take a tent when they go out into nature for recreation. However, to be a skillful survivalist, you cannot rely on store-bought shelters because you never know when you will not have access to one.

You have to have proper shelter when you're outdoors.[23]

Different environments need different shelters. To be adaptable in all situations, you have to be aware of multiple construction techniques and the many kinds of structure options you have. Each ecosystem has a unique personality that responds to the actions you take. You cannot do the same thing in the rainforest as you would in the snow of Siberia. Using what is available is the key to survival. Therefore, you must learn how to look at the world around you as a "natural" hardware store you can use to find raw materials. By adjusting how you think about nature, you will find that everything you need is right at your fingertips.

Why Shelter Is Important

There are many reasons why shelter is typically the first thing on the list to sort out for survival. Firstly, you need protection from the elements, sun, rain, and wind. Secondly, especially at night, you must find a way to maintain your body temperature. The normal body temperature for a person is 98.6 F. If your temperature drops below 95 F, you are experiencing hypothermia, which means your body temperature is too low and you are in danger. So, keeping yourself warm is closely tied to keeping yourself alive.

An elevated shelter, especially in the jungle, can protect you from snakes and insects on the ground. Therefore, a shelter is not just for your warmth but is also extremely important for your safety. Furthermore, having a certain level of comfort allows you to sleep better. A lack of sleep messes with your mind, so you will not be as sharp, and your responses will be much slower. In the wilderness, you need mental clarity to make good decisions that will enhance your probability of survival.

A shelter can also help you hide from predators. Building a discreet shelter that blends in with its background could help you avoid drawing attention from any animals that could harm you. Although camouflaging your shelter will not keep you 100 percent safe, it gives you an edge that could swing the odds of escaping an attack in your favor. If you are in a dangerous area where predators are roaming, your best bet is to stay hidden.

Your campsite is the hub of your survival that you will return to regularly to eat and sleep. Your shelter is the wilderness home that you will use as a place to keep a fire going to cook and boil water, as well as a place where you can store much-needed survival materials. You need a place to regroup and return to so you can keep your sanity in the wild.

Your shelter gives you peace of mind so you can remain calm and operate at your highest level. Therefore, when you are in the bush, you should work from building a shelter and then cater to your other needs. Shelter construction is a high-energy activity, so you probably want to get it out of the way as soon as possible.

Key Principles of Shelter Construction

You may be looking at your cleverly built shelter made from natural materials and giving yourself a pat on the back for a job well done, but there are some boxes you must tick before you attempt to use your shelter. A leaking, cold shelter may be better than nothing. Still, you can exponentially increase your comfort and safety by ensuring your shelter is wind-resistant, waterproof, and insulated to keep you warm. Additionally, you also want to take measures to keep as many bugs and spiders away as possible.

Insulation

Insulation means keeping warmth in while it's cold outside. Even in more temperate regions, temperatures can quickly drop at night. Cold weather can be a death sentence, so insulation must be taken seriously. Bark, leaves, wood chips, and plants can be layered strategically to keep the cold out. Do not sleep directly on the ground; this is a quick way to lose heat. Use a wood floor made with branches, and layer leaves and branches at the bottom and top to keep you elevated off the ground. Your insulation material should cover any gaps in the structure so the heat from your breath and body can be kept in the shelter while the cold air from outside is kept out. Use what you have available, so blankets, sleeping bags, cushions, clothing, and even newspapers can be used to insulate yourself.

Waterproofing

Not many things on the planet are as bad as cold and wet moisture preventing you from sleeping. Whether it is dew in the early morning or the pouring rain in a forest, making your shelter waterproof will keep you warm and comfortable. Waterproofing follows a similar blueprint to insulation because they both use similar materials. Strategically positioning your camp where water doesn't gather is the first step to waterproofing your shelter. Next, you want materials you can layer and weave together so the gaps in your shelter's wooden frame can be closed. Moss and pine needles are great for waterproofing, especially in cold places where it often snows. You can also use grass, reeds, and leaves to keep all water out. Sometimes, everything does not go as planned, so keep some extra material nearby to patch your shelter as needed and carry a tarp in your kit.

Having a waterproof tent will keep the rain at bay and you can have a restful sleep.[24]

Wind Protection

Wind protection works hand in hand with insulation and waterproofing. Again, the materials you choose to shelter yourself from wind must fill all the openings in your shelter. A tip for wind protection is keeping the entryway to your shelter small because less air will be able to get in. Another useful trick to remember is to use cords to tie down your insulation material so the wind does not blow it away. Everything in your shelter must be solid so that the weather does not destroy the structure. Use your surroundings to your advantage and build close to a rock formation or in between trees so that your habitat can help you block the strong wind.

Natural Shelters

Sometimes, it is easier to find a shelter than it is to build one. You are trying to work smart – not hard – in the bush. Using what's already available is the key that everyone with survival knowledge must fully understand. Look around and see what you can use to your advantage. Be creative and think outside of the box. When you find natural shelters, you must be vigilant because they may already be an animal or insect owner of that shelter. Your senses should always be on high alert because nature can be unforgiving. Being in the wild is fun, but your safety should always be your first concern. Look for a dry place that shields you from wind and where you can make a fire to keep predators away. Make sure to clean the structure before you use it because there may be unwanted creepy crawlies looking to enter through cracks and holes.

You can find shelter in nature to keep you safe.[25]

Below is a list of natural shelters you can use to save time and energy. Be on the lookout for the following naturally occurring structures:
- Caves
- Rock formations
- Hollow trees
- Fallen trees
- Thick bushes or shrubs
- Cliffs
- Evergreen trees
- Low land formations
- Overhangs

Building a Shelter

Now that you understand the principles and importance of building a shelter, you need some practical tips and ideas for how you can go about constructing the best shelter in any situation. Wilderness shelters are easy to build, low-effort, and use materials that are readily available around you. You do not need anything fancy; it just needs to be functional. Remember, when you spend time in nature, you should leave things the way you found them, so always clean up your campsite before you leave to respect the plants and animals that receive you as their guest.

Lean-to Shelter

A lean-to structure is simple to build and can be put up in various places.[96]

A lean-to structure is simple to build and can be used in various places.

- First, you need to find either a rock face or two strong trees that are close together.
- If you are using a rock face, find straight branches about the same size and lean them against the hard surface.
- Next, tie smaller sticks horizontally across the sticks you have leaned vertically against the rock face.
- Lastly, fill in the gaps with insulation like leaves or moss.
- If you are using two trees, there is one extra step. You must secure a long branch horizontally between two trees. You can repeat the same steps as you would for a rock face by angling sticks from the ground against the stick you secure at about your waist height.
- You will then fill the gaps with leaves and greenery to provide insulation.
- Don't forget to insulate the ground as well.

A-Frame Shelter

This shelter is a little more complicated than the lean-to, but it has the added advantage of camouflaging the shelter well and having a bit more insulation for colder environments.

- Find a thick, strong branch to use as a ridge pole. Lean this branch against a strong tree and tie it down with some cord.
- Next, collect more branches that you will lean on the center pole you created with the first branch. Ensure the sticks are angled to firmly stabilize and tie them down on the ground.
- Collect debris like leaves, pine branches, or moss to insulate your shelter. Crawl into the shelter and pack additional debris in the doorway to seal you up inside snugly and comfortably.

Tarp Shelters

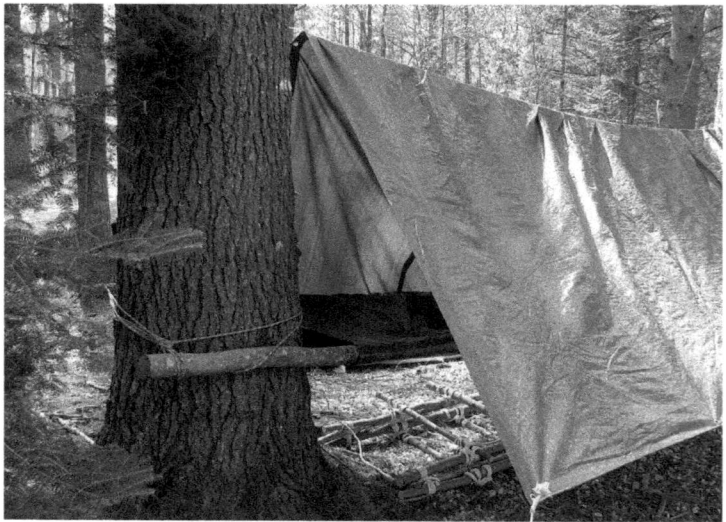

A tarp shelter is one of the easiest structures to build.[27]

A tarp shelter is one of the easiest structures to build. Carrying a tarp with you in the wilderness can be useful for shelter and collecting water. Tarps are more waterproof and warmer than shelters, using debris like sticks and leaves for insulation. Therefore, a tarp is an amazing survival tool.

- Start by laying your tarp flat on the ground and securing the corners with heavy rocks.
- Find a strong stick and place it upright in the middle of your tarp. You can dig a hole for the stick to secure it better.
- Lastly, insulate your floor with wood and branches to keep your body from absorbing the cold from the ground.

Emergency Shelter with Limited Resources

You will not always find everything you need for your shelter, so you must use what you have on hand. All of the shelters described above can be created with limited resources. Feel free to get creative. You can use the materials you have on you for a shelter. Pollution sometimes provides useful materials like plastic or paper that can be used as frames or insulation in a shelter. A tarp or a raincoat can also be repurposed as waterproofing. The wilderness and emergency survival situations demand that you use anything you have on hand to your benefit. You just have to look at your resources with an engineer's eyes.

Choosing the Best Campsite

Choosing a great campsite to build a structure is half of the job. A few considerations must be kept in mind when finding the perfect spot. Firstly, ensure that you are at least 200 hundred meters away from any water source to prevent flooding. Check the drainage of the campsite to ensure that water flows away well and does not gather in that spot. Try to find a solid surface like gravel or hard ground. You want a campsite with minimal pests and away from any animal homes. Look around to make sure that there are no rocks or trees that can fall on you. The best campsite is where it is dry with some protection from the wind. If you are in an area where it is extremely hot, finding a shady spot could also be helpful.

Section 5: Firecraft

Having the skill to build a fire is something everyone should learn. It's not just helpful for starting a campfire. It can be used in so many different ways. Imagine you're out in the wild, and the night is getting dark and scary. That's when a fire can be your best friend.

First of all, a fire can keep you safe and cozy. It's like a warm hug from Mother Nature, keeping you toasty when it's chilly outside. Plus, the crackling flames can scare away any curious wild animals considering visiting your campsite.

It's like a warm hug from Mother Nature, keeping you toasty when it's chilly outside.[38]

But that's not all. A fire can also be a secret message to your friends or rescuers in the dark. If you need help, a blazing fire sends a beacon saying, "I'm here, come find me!" So, in some situations, a fire can literally save your life.

However, building a fire is more challenging than it may seem. It needs three things to work: air, heat, and fuel. However, here's the tricky part. It's super hard to get all those things to cooperate on a rainy day, and if you're tired and a bit scared, it becomes even tougher.

Imagine using a whole bunch of matches and still being unable to start a fire. What would you do then? That's the adventure of fire-making. Sometimes it's easy, and sometimes it's a real challenge, but once you master it, you'll feel like a wilderness expert!

Preparing the Fire Area

Preparing your fire area is important to ensure a successful and safe campfire.

1. Choosing the Right Spot

First, you should pick a location that's already safe for making a fire. Look for places like the top of a big rock or a sandy area. It's best to find a spot that's sheltered from the wind. If you can, find a big boulder or rock behind which you can place your fire area. This way, more of the fire's heat will bounce back to keep you warm.

2. Clear the Way

To be smart and safe, clear a circle at least 10 feet wide for your fire area. That means removing anything that can catch fire easily, like leaves, grass, and pine needles. This will prevent the fire from spreading where you don't want it to. Dig a shallow hole in the ground to create a fire pit if you can. This makes your fire safer and makes it easier to light when there's a breeze. If digging a pit isn't an option, you can make a ring of rocks around your fire area. These rocks will help contain the flames and stay warm even after the fire dies.

3. Snowy Situations

If you're in a snowy area, you can't just plop a fire on top of the snow. You'll need to create a sturdy foundation for your fire. Gather logs or large sticks to make a deck. This way, your fire won't melt into the snow.

You need to have a good foundation to start a fire in the snow.[29]

Materials for Your Fire

Once your spot is set up, it's time to collect the materials you need for your fire. To keep a fire going strong all night, you'll need more wood than you might think. You'll need three main types of wood: tinder, kindling, and logs.

- **Tinder:** This is the stuff you light first to start the fire. It needs to be super dry and easy to catch fire. The dryer your tinder, the better it works. You can use things like dry leaves, paper, or even special fire-starting materials you might have.

- **Kindling:** These are thin sticks and small branches that you feed the fire to help it grow. They're like the appetizer for your fire, getting it ready for the big logs. Make sure your kindling is dry, too.

- **Logs:** The main event! These bigger pieces of wood keep your fire burning steadily. They provide the lasting warmth and light you need during your camping adventure.

Tinder Types

When building a fire, having the right tinder can make your life much easier. Think of tinder as the magical stuff that catches fire first and helps you get that cozy campfire going. Below, explore different types of tinder you can use:

1. Carry Your Tinder

If you're well-prepared and have a survival kit, you can save time and effort by taking some tinder with you. Good tinder materials to pack include fine steel wool, shredded paper, waxed paper, or small pieces of fatwood (which comes from a resinous tree). You can even check your pockets for dryer lint; it's usually dry and makes excellent tinder.

2. Nature's Tinder

If you didn't bring your own tinder, and it's a wet day, don't worry. Mother Nature has you covered. Look for dry pine needles, grass, or dried rabbit or deer droppings. These can work as natural tinder. You can also find small pieces of dry wood or bark. And if the ground isn't helping, you can turn to punk. Punk is rotted wood inside trees that have been dead for a while. Birch or cedar tree bark can be shredded and used as tinder. Birch trees have white, papery bark, and cedar trees look like redwood or pine trees but have flat leaves. Break them up or shred them to create a loose bundle.

Hunting for Firewood

Now, it's time to find the bigger pieces for your fire. Search for firewood in places protected from the weather, like under a big tree or beneath a piece of bark. Once you've got your fire going, you can put damp wood near the fire to dry it out for later use.

Building Your Fire

There are many ways to build a fire, but they all start by lighting small bits of dry tinder. Arrange the tinder so the flames are shielded from the wind but can still get some oxygen. You can make a teepee shape with your tinder and small sticks or lean a bundle of tinder against a log. When you see flames in your tinder, gently blow on the fire to add oxygen and carefully feed it with small kindling sticks. Add one or two sticks at a time until your fire burns nicely. Once you have a strong fire, you can add larger sticks and, eventually, logs.

Fire Starters and Fire-Starting Materials

Once you've got your tinder ready, the next step is to ignite it, and you need reliable tools to do that. Some survival books discuss starting fires with flint, fire plows, or bow drills. These methods can be fun to learn but are not very practical when you're cold, scared, wet, and alone in the woods. You need quick, easy, and foolproof ways to start a fire.

1. Store-Bought Fire Starters

You can find some fantastic fire-starting products in camping stores. Here are a couple of them:

- **Waterproof Matches:** These matches are lifesavers, as they light easily, even in wet conditions. Just make sure to keep the striker paper dry by packing them in a sealed container.
- **Disposable Lighters:** These are cheap and usually work even if they get wet. You can dry it out if yours gets wet, and it should work fine. Carrying both waterproof matches and a lighter whenever you go hiking is a good idea.

2. Using the Sun's Power

On sunny days, you can use sunlight to start a fire.[30]

On sunny days, you can use sunlight to start a fire. A small magnifying glass or even a pair of eyeglasses can do the trick. In fact, anything that reflects sunlight can help create a fire. People have even ignited fires using glass bowls on wood decks, crystals in windows, or drinking glasses left on windowsills. You are harnessing the power of the sun!

3. **DIY Fire-Starting Materials**

If you don't have store-bought fire starters, don't worry. You can make your own with simple things you may have:

- **Tortilla Chips:** Hold a flame from a match or lighter under a tortilla chip for a few seconds, and it will catch fire. Light-colored chips with less seasoning work best.
- **Toilet Paper and Candle Wax**: Coat individual toilet paper squares with melted candle wax. These catch fire quickly and burn steadily.
- **Cotton Balls and Petroleum Jelly:** Dip cotton balls in petroleum jelly (like Vaseline). They catch fire immediately and burn strongly for quite a while.
- **Fire Paste:** Sold in tubes, you squeeze it onto wood and light it. It ignites instantly.
- **Fuel Tablets**: Various solid fuel tablets that burn well and provide enough heat to cook over are available.
- **Magnesium Block Scrapings**: You can buy blocks of magnesium with a flint edge. Shave some magnesium flakes onto your tinder, then strike the flint with a knife to create sparks that set the magnesium flakes on fire. It works even when damp.

4. **Improvise with What You Have**

If you didn't bring fire-starting materials, think about what you did bring that could be used as a substitute. Do you have lint in your pocket, tissues, a candy bar wrapper, or a piece of paper you can tear off and shred?

Basic Fire-Starting Methods

- **Tinder Bundle:** Gather dry leaves, grass, and small sticks. Make a little bundle out of them. Now, use matches or a lighter to set the bundle on fire. Blow on it gently to make the flames grow.
- **Fire Starter Kit:** Get a special kit with waterproof matches, cotton balls, and a striker. Learn how to light the matches and use the cotton balls as fire starters.
- **Magnifying Glass:** Use a magnifying glass to catch the sun's rays on sunny days. Aim the glass at a pile of dry stuff like leaves or paper and watch it start to smoke and catch fire. Magic!

You can use a magnifying glass to start a fire.[81]

- **Candle and Tinder:** Light a candle with a grown-up's help and use the candle's flame to start a fire in a safe and controlled way. This helps you learn without touching big flames.

Intermediate Fire-Building Techniques

- **Teepee Fire Lay:** Arrange small sticks in a teepee shape around your tinder bundle. This lets the air get in and makes your fire grow. Add bigger sticks as your fire gets bigger.

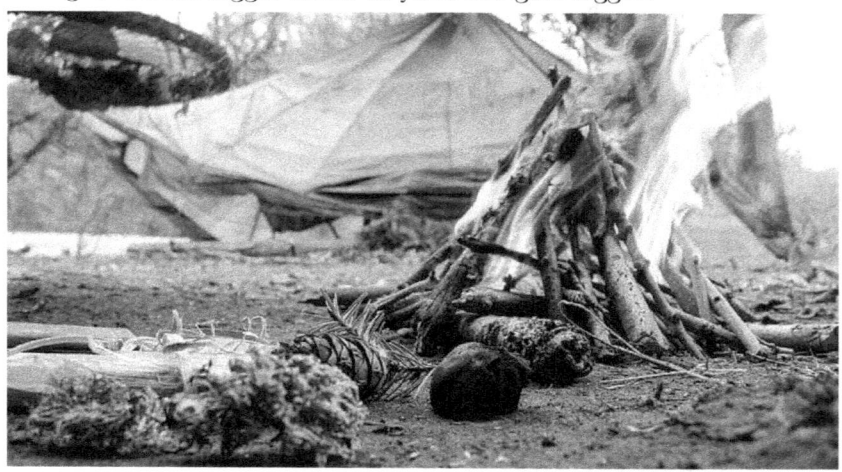

Arrange small sticks in a teepee shape around your tinder bundle.[82]

- **Log Cabin Fire Lay:** Make a little log cabin out of your sticks with your tinder bundle inside. Light the bundle, and the log cabin falls apart as it burns, adding more sticks to the fire.

Make a little log cabin out of your sticks with your tinder bundle inside.[33]

- **Lean-To Fire Lay:** Build a little shelter with sticks, leaving one side open like a tent. Put your tinder inside, light it up, and the fire will catch on. This is good for windy days.

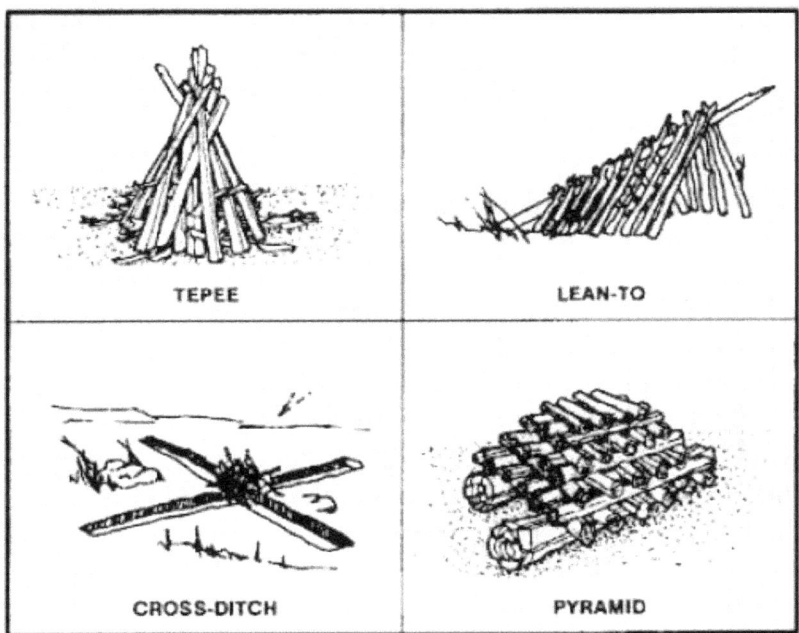

Build a little shelter with sticks, leaving one side open like a tent.[34]

Advanced Fire-Starting Methods (with Grown-Up Help)

- **Fire Starter Tools**: These tools make hot sparks when you scrape them. A grown-up can help you use them to light your tinder.
- **Flint and Steel**: Strike a piece of special rock (like flint) against a steel striker to make sparks. Use the sparks to light your tinder.
- **Bow Drill:** The bow drill is like magic. It needs a spindle, a hearth board, a bow, and a socket. By moving the bow fast, you can heat and light the tinder. It takes practice!
- **Fire by Friction**: These methods involve rubbing things together to create heat, like the hand drill or fire plow. They're tricky and need a lot of practice. Grown-ups can help you learn.

Disclaimer: Always have an adult present before starting a fire.

Staying Warm and Staying Safe

To keep warm at night, you can heat rocks next to the fire and place them under your clothes or in your shelter. Be careful because they'll be hot! Don't put rocks that have been sitting in water or that have small pockets or cracks into the fire. These can explode when heated. Always be cautious when picking up rocks, as you may find unexpected guests like rattlesnakes or scorpions hiding underneath. Use a stick to flip rocks over first.

If you're stranded for more than a day or have some extra time, you can build a big fire in a trench the size of your body. Once it burns down to coals, cover the entire fire bed with sand or dirt. Put green branches on top, and you'll have a warm bed. These branches prevent you from accidentally exposing the coals while you sleep. Another way to make a heated bed is by building a fire on a large rock you plan to sleep on. After brushing off the coals, the rock stays warm for hours.

Remember to extinguish your campfire before leaving. Pour water on it if possible, and stir it with a stick to ensure it's out. If you don't have water, cover the fire with a thick layer of dirt or sand. Ensure the fire is entirely out before you go. This is vital because many forest and brush fires have started from campfires that weren't correctly extinguished and which smoldered for hours.

Section 6: Water and Edibles

In this section, you will learn about the most essential items in bushcraft: water and edibles. You will discover their importance, how to find and identify them, and how to prepare these items safely. With these invaluable skills, you can survive almost anywhere!

Why Is Water Vital for Survival?

You must always keep a water bottle with you or have a water source with you at all times.[35]

Going without water for too long causes you to become seriously dehydrated, which can be fatal. You must always keep a water bottle with you or always have a water source with you. In hot, arid desert environments, the consequences of dehydration are much more serious than in milder environments. Even mild dehydration can negatively impact your mental and physical well-being, which may cause you to make poor decisions.

If you are in snowy surroundings, dehydration may not be a huge concern. You can always eat snow to hydrate yourself. However, you must be cautious, as eating too much snow can cause your core body temperature to drop. It should not be a problem if you are traveling or physically active. If your body temperature drops, you can always engage in physical activities like squats or jumping jacks. You must always try to melt snow if possible. If your body temperature drops below a certain level, you can become a victim of hypothermia. Here are some sources where you can find water in the wilderness:

Gravity

Gravity is your friend when it comes to finding water in the wilderness. You must look for water in the lowest elevation areas, such as valleys. Usually, the water is drained and collected in the form of a pool. Even if there is no sign of water there, you can dig the ground to reveal some water that will gather in the hole you've dug. You may also find water in green areas with plants, as that is also a sign of the presence of water.

Rain

If you are in a rainforest, you will find water everywhere. You will find it collected in the corners of the forest. However, it is best to boil it before drinking it. If you come across fresh pockets of rainwater, you can drink it with a straw made from a plant or bamboo. You can filter out big particles using grass, sand, or cloth fabric. However, it will not filter out the bacteria or pathogens.

Dew

Morning dew is also a great way to collect water in areas where the nights are cold and the days are warm. The hot air absorbs a lot of moisture, so when the night falls, the air cannot hold it, so it is condensed into dew. You can use tree bark to store water as it is waterproof and does not absorb water. You can also use clothes to absorb the dew drops and wring them into the boiling pot. You can wrap these clothes around your legs and walk through the grass to absorb dew from the grass. You can then wring that water into a pot and boil it for safe consumption.

Vegetation

If you are looking for water, it is always good to look around green vegetation. If you come across green foliage, you can know for certain that there is water there. Even if you don't see any water there, you can try digging the ground, and it will eventually cause water to come up. Moreover, a place with animals is another sign of the presence of water.

Risks of Drinking Untreated Water

It is imperative to consume safe drinking water while you are on your outdoor adventure. However, in the absence of it, you must refrain from drinking unhealthy water. You must not drink directly from natural raw water sources, as it can be full of bacteria and viruses. There is a risk of getting dangerous waterborne viral diseases like rotavirus and hepatitis A. You can also feel nauseated and get stomach cramps and aches from drinking dirty water. Moreover, you can get parasites, worms, or diarrhea from drinking from these unhealthy sources. This is why you must boil water before consuming it.

Water Purification Methods

Once you have sourced and collected your water, always purify it before consumption. There are many ways you can purify or filter your water in nature:

Boiling

Boiling water is the safest and simplest way of making water safe for consumption.[36]

Boiling water is the safest and simplest way of making water safe for consumption. It eliminates all the bacteria and viruses but not chemicals. If you can access fire and wood, boil water before drinking it. You must boil water for a longer time if you're on elevation. You can boil water in a metal pot or nesting cup. Do not use insulated metal cups, or you will burn a hole in them.

Coarse Filtration

You can filter water by coarse filtration using a brown bag, a bandana, or a cloth to remove deposits and turbidity. Coarse filtration reduces bacteria or viruses if attached to dirt but does not filter out the largest pathogenic organisms. This method to clean water is used before chemical methods to clean more efficiently.

Microfiltration

Using pumps, ceramic filters, or gravity systems, you can employ microfiltration techniques to remove large pathogenic organisms, including protozoa, without using heat. However, it may not be effective for viruses and bacteria.

Chemical Sterilization

Under adult supervision, you can also use chemical sterilization methods such as chlorine and iodine.

Chlorine

Chlorine helps remove bacteria and viruses but does not get rid of protozoan cysts.

Iodine

Iodine is excellent for cleaning turbid water and removing protozoa, bacteria, and viruses.

Ultraviolet Techniques

You can use ultraviolet techniques to clean your water and remove bacteria, viruses, and protozoa. These devices, however, require the water to be filtered and clear. Also, these devices may require batteries.

Wild Edibles

The world is filled with edibles. Wherever you go, there is a high chance you'll find edible plants around you, such as nuts, roots, berries, flowers, seeds, fungi, foliage, etc. Often, the whole plant is edible. Before you embark on your foraging journey, learn how to consume and identify plants. Do not eat anything that may seem edible. Certain toxic plants have a similar appearance to other plants. Keep a book or guide of edible plants with you to recognize the ones you can eat.

General Rules for Foraging

Here are some general rules you must follow when foraging for food:
1. An animal eating it does not make the food safe for you to eat.
2. Do not consume a part of a plant without asking an adult.
3. If a plant is smelly, avoid it.
4. Poison ivy and other plants that grow in groups of three should not be eaten.
5. Plants that are found near busy roadsides or in developed regions should be thoroughly cleaned to prevent pollution from pesticides.
6. Not all plants are safe to be consumed raw.
7. Never consume rotting fruit or berries.
8. Ensure you are not allergic to a fruit, vegetable, or berry. Consume new plants slowly and one by one.
9. Wait a while before eating more so you know if there is any negative impact.
10. Always follow the Leave No Trace philosophy to ensure that your surroundings are pristine for the enjoyment of future visitors.

Common Edible Plants

These plants are easy to identify and have at least one part you can consume safely. It is easy to locate these options throughout the United States. Pick up a local guide to identify and select your favorite wild food plants.

1. Nasturtium

Look for nasturtium near your home before you embark on your outdoor adventure. It's a lovely spicy plant that can be orange, yellow, or red. It can easily be found in gardens or parks and in the native land of South America. All parts of this plant, from seeds to leaves, are edible and rich in vitamins.

Look for nasturtium near your home before you embark on your outdoor adventure.[87]

2. Prickly Pear Cactus

You can find food even in the desert. Mexico and the American Southwest are home to prickly pear cacti. Its arms are paddle-shaped, and it contains vivid pink fruit. Before eating it, you have to peel its skin and remove its spines. Its fruit is widely used to make fresh pink juice.

3. Morel

Delicious mushrooms that grow in the spring are called morels. Ensure you don't stumble onto a "false morel," which can trick the uninformed eye and is somewhat harmful.

4. Pine Nuts

Pine nuts are incredibly delicious and nourishing, but they need a lot of time to gather. This is why you must not consider them your go-to survival situation. These are seeds, not nuts, and are found in pinecones. The seeds of pinyon pines grow all over the American Southwest.

5. Dandelion

Dandelions are edible and can be found everywhere. The leaves should be consumed young because they eventually turn bitter and include vitamins K and A. The mature leaves and roots must be cooked before eating for improved flavor. The golden blossom can be added to a salad or eaten raw.

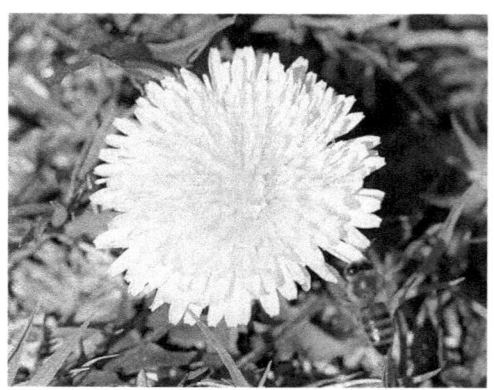

Dandelions are edible and can be found everywhere.[38]

Plants to Avoid

You must learn how to identify edible plants from poisonous ones. Awareness of them will help you and your pets stay safe, as they can also be found in your backyard and parks.

1. Horse Nettle

The fruit of the horse nettle resembles cherry tomatoes because it is a member of the eggplant or tomato family. The fruit may seem appetizing but is toxic; therefore, you should not eat it. It is found in the American South. It consists of spines and tastes bitter.

2. Doll's Eyes

These berries are white with black dots in the center. They resemble a doll's eyes, hence the name. The whole plant is toxic and can be found in the eastern side of the US.

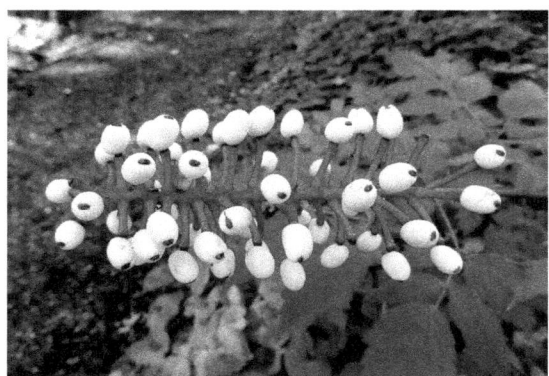

These berries are white with black dots in the center.[39]

3. Poison Ivy

Humans cannot eat poison ivy even though birds eat its seeds and deer consume its leaves. It gives people an itchy rash, so learn to identify it as it grows in shrubs, fields, parks, and vines.

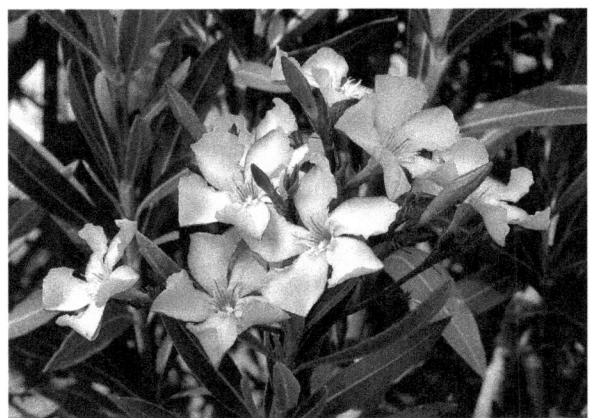

4. Oleander

Oleander features lovely blossoms and smells delicious, like apricots. However, all parts of this plant are toxic and can kill you. They are found in Florida, Texas, and California.

Oleander features lovely blossoms and smells delicious, like apricots.[40]

5. Manchineel

Manchineel trees are extremely dangerous. Consuming its apple-like fruit can prove to be fatal. It is also called the tree of death. It is found in the Florida Keys and southern Florida. It grows wild along swampy or coastal locations in Central America, Mexico, and the Caribbean.

How to Identify and Assess the Edibility of Wildlife

You should know how to identify and assess the edibility of wild animals and insects. You must always be under adult supervision while dealing with wild animals and learn about their species, habitats, and behaviors, especially those around the water source. Be aware of edible and non-edible animal parts. Furthermore, see if you can determine what illnesses an animal may have. Lastly, always respect nature and animals and avoid disturbing them.

Cooking Methods and Preservation Techniques

Learning to cook and preserve food is a rewarding life skill that will help you become more self-reliant. Here are some cooking and preservation techniques.

Cooking Techniques
Campfire Cooking

You can build a campfire and use skewers for roasting marshmallows. You may also cook food like hot dogs, vegetables, and small pieces of meat over an open flame by putting it on sticks or skewers.

Solar Cooking

You can use a solar oven to cook food. You can align the oven with the sun to cook things like smores.

Boiling and Grilling

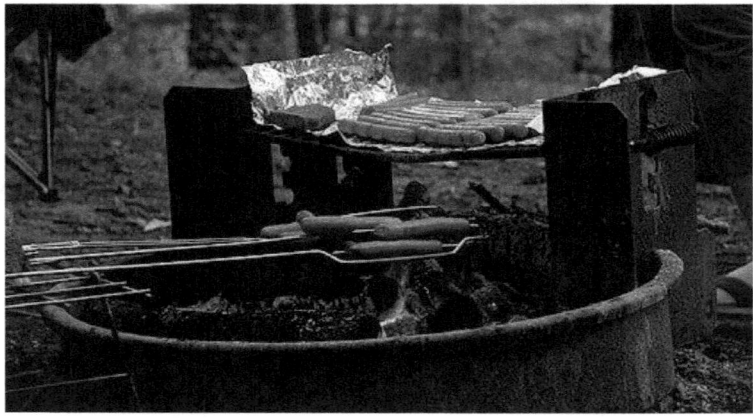

Grilling can help you cook meat or vegetables over the flames.[41]

You can boil water to cook pasta, rice, and soup. Grilling can help you cook meat or vegetables over the flames.

Preservation Techniques

Drying

You can air dry your fruit and vegetables to avoid spoilage and also store them in containers to use in the future.

Smoking

You can smoke your meat or fish to preserve it. Do it with an adult, as it can be complicated.

Canning

You can prepare jams and pickles for canning. You need sterilized jars for proper sealing.

Section 7: First Aid Basics

Imagine you're out in the wilderness, surrounded by towering trees, winding rivers, and the sounds of birds and insects. It's a thrilling adventure but can also be where things sometimes go differently than planned. That's why you need to know all about first aid, especially when there's no hospital nearby or when it might take time for medical assistance to arrive.

Far from Help

Sometimes, you can be far from towns or cities when exploring the wild. Therefore, if something goes wrong, you may not be able to get to a hospital quickly. Knowing first aid means you can help yourself and your friends until the grown-ups arrive.

Quick Thinking

When accidents happen, they don't wait. You must know what to do right away. First aid teaches you to think fast and act smart in emergencies, like when someone gets hurt or suddenly feels sick.

Nature's Surprises

The wilderness is full of surprises – some are amazing, like spotting a deer, and some are a bit scary, like getting stung by a bee or tripping on a rock. First aid helps you handle these surprises, whether a small scratch or a bigger problem, like knowing what to do if you meet a wild animal.

Be a Helper

When you know first aid, you can be a hero. If someone's hurt or in trouble, you can be the one to make things better. It feels great to help others and make sure they're safe.

Safety with Friends

If you're out exploring with your friends, it's not just about keeping yourself safe – it's about keeping them safe, too. First aid skills help you care for your buddies and ensure everyone has a fun and safe adventure.

Stopping Small Problems

Sometimes, a small problem can turn big if you need help figuring out what to do, but with first aid, you can stop minor problems from worsening. For example, if you get a cut, knowing how to clean and bandage it can stop it from getting infected.

So, learning first aid in the wilderness is more than just knowing how to put on a bandage. It's about preparing for the unexpected, helping others, and ensuring you have the best adventure ever. It's a life skill that keeps you and your friends safe while you explore the incredible world of nature.

Accessing Injuries and Illnesses

Step 1: Stay Calm

In any emergency, the first thing to do is to keep a clear and calm mind. Take a deep breath and try not to panic. This will help you think more clearly and make better decisions.

Step 2: Check for Dangers

Before you approach anyone who needs help, take a good look around. Make sure the area is safe for you to enter to avoid making a bad situation worse. Check for slippery rocks, thorny bushes, or other potential hazards. If it's not safe, then don't go any further. Your safety is essential, too.

Step 3: Assess the Situation

Approach the person who needs help, but do it carefully. If they're unconscious, gently shake their shoulders and talk to them. Ask loudly, "Are you okay?" If they don't respond, this is a severe situation. It's time to get help from an adult or call for assistance if you have a phone.

Step 4: Ask Questions

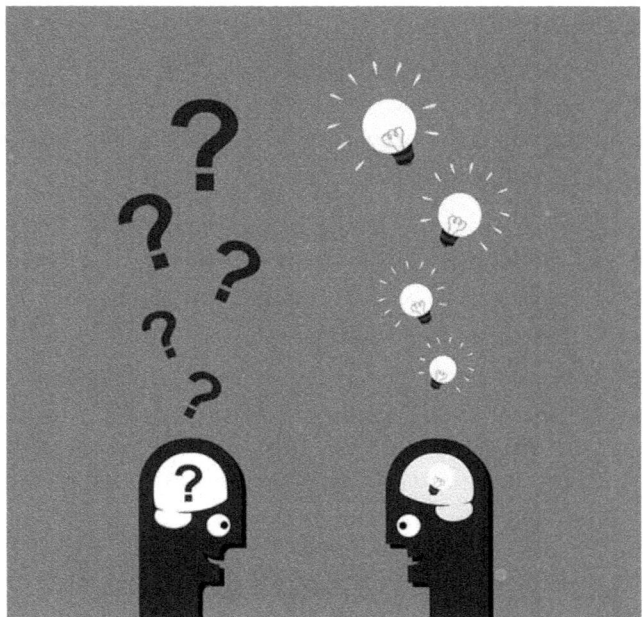

If the person is conscious and able to talk, ask them what happened.[42]

If the person is conscious and able to talk, ask them what happened. "Can you tell me what happened?" Listen carefully to their answers. It will give you essential information about their condition.

Step 5: Look for Injuries

Carefully check the person's body for any injuries. Look for cuts, scrapes, bruises, or anything that looks unusual. When you find an injury, pay close attention. If there's bleeding, that's a top priority to take care of. Use a clean cloth or bandage to stop the bleeding and protect the area.

Step 6: Check for Illness

Sometimes, people feel sick in the wilderness. They may have symptoms like dizziness, a headache, nausea, or extreme heat or cold. Ask them about how they're feeling and what they're experiencing. Look for signs like sweating, paleness, or redness of the face. These signs can give you clues about what might be wrong.

Step 7: Prioritize Care

Now, you need to decide what needs your attention most urgently. Remember the three Ps: Preserve Life, Prevent Further Injury, and Promote Recovery.

Preserve Life: If someone is not breathing or their heart is not beating, you need to start CPR (if you know how) or get an adult to help immediately. This is the most critical because it's about saving their life.

Prevent Further Injury: If there is bleeding, apply pressure to stop it. If someone has a broken bone, try to keep it from moving. Ensure the person is safe from any other dangers present in the area.

Promote Recovery: After addressing immediate dangers, your next goal is to keep the person comfortable. For example, if they're cold, provide them with a blanket. If they're thirsty, offer water. If they have a headache, suggest they rest and take deep breaths.

Step 8: Get Help

In severe situations, informing an adult and calling for help is crucial. If you have a phone, use it to call emergency services or get in touch with someone who can help. If there's no phone signal, send someone to find a park ranger or another responsible person nearby.

Remember, it's crucial to stay within your comfort zone. If the situation is too big or risky for you to handle, find an adult and let them take charge. Knowing how to assess injuries and illnesses in the wilderness is like becoming a real-life hero and nature detective. You gather clues, make wise decisions, and help those in need. These skills make your outdoor adventures safer and more enjoyable for everyone involved.

First Aid Supplies to Include

A well-prepared bushcraft kit should include essential first aid supplies to address common wilderness injuries and ailments. Here's a list of basic first-aid supplies for your bushcraft kit:

Adhesive Bandages

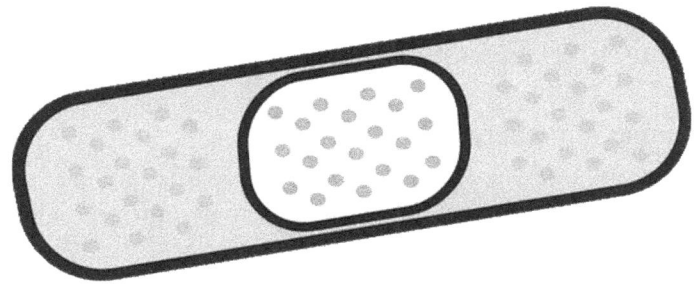

They are often called "band-aids," small, sticky strips with a padded center.[43]

They are often called "band-aids," small, sticky strips with a padded center. They cover and protect small wounds like cuts, blisters, or abrasions. Different sizes are available to match the wound's dimensions and location.

Sterile Gauze Pads

Gauze pads are made of sterile, woven fabric for dressing larger wounds, burns, or deep cuts. They keep the wound clean and help prevent infection. Gauze rolls are used to secure dressings in place, especially for wrapping or covering larger injuries.

Medical Tape

Medical tape is a special adhesive tape designed for medical applications. It's used to secure gauze, bandages, or other dressings in place, ensuring they remain clean and firmly attached to the skin.

Antiseptic Wipes or Solution

Wipes or solutions contain disinfectants for cleaning wounds and preventing infection. Wiping the area around a cut or scrape reduces the risk of harmful bacteria entering the wound, promoting faster healing.

Scissors and Tweezers

Used for cutting medical tape, clothing, or bandages to the desired length. Tweezers are used for safely and accurately removing splinters, thorns, or other foreign objects from wounds without using your fingers, which may introduce infection.

Elastic Bandage

Elastic bandages are stretchy and support sprained or strained limbs, such as ankles or wrists. They help reduce swelling and immobilize injured areas to prevent further damage.

Pain Relievers

Acetaminophen or ibuprofen can alleviate minor discomfort caused by headaches, muscle aches, or minor pain from injuries. They can make a patient feel more comfortable.

Antihistamine (for Allergic Reactions)

Antihistamines, often available as pills or creams, are used to manage allergic reactions, insect stings, or mild allergic symptoms. They work by reducing itching and swelling associated with allergies.

Cotton Swabs

Cotton balls and swabs are versatile and can be used for various medical tasks, such as cleaning wounds, applying ointments or creams, or helping with hygiene in the field.

Thermometer

A thermometer is a device for measuring body temperature. Elevated temperature can indicate fever or illness, essential to monitor in the wilderness.

Tweezers

Tweezers are fine-tipped, precision instruments for safely removing splinters, thorns, or other foreign objects embedded in the skin. You must keep them clean and sterile.

Emergency Blanket

An emergency blanket, or a space blanket, is a compact, lightweight, and reflective sheet that helps retain body heat. It can provide warmth and shelter in cases of exposure or shock.

Tourniquet (for Severe Bleeding)

A tourniquet should be used only in extreme cases when other means cannot control severe bleeding."

A tourniquet should be used only in extreme cases when other means cannot control severe bleeding. Proper training is necessary to avoid complications when applying a tourniquet.

Cleansing Soap or Hand Sanitizer

Proper hand hygiene prevents contamination of wounds and equipment. Use cleansing soap or hand sanitizer before treating injuries to reduce the risk of infection.

First Aid Manual or Guide

A first-aid manual provides detailed instructions on administering first-aid in various situations. Have one with you in case you encounter unfamiliar injuries or medical issues.

Emergency Contact Information

Include a list of emergency contacts, such as family members, friends, or park rangers. This information is vital if you or your group requires assistance in a wilderness emergency.

Prescription Medications (If Necessary)

If you or someone in your group needs prescription medications for a medical condition, ensure these medications are included in your first aid kit.

Remember that your bushcraft first aid kit should be customized based on the specific needs of your adventure and the number of people in your group. Regularly check and replenish supplies as they are used or expired. Learning how to use these supplies effectively through first aid training or courses will benefit you in a wilderness setting.

Wound Care

Cuts and Scrapes

1. **Wash Hands:** First, wash your hands with soap and water.
2. **Clean the Wound:** Clean the cut or scrape with mild soap and water. Use a clean cloth or gauze.
3. **Stop Bleeding:** If it's bleeding, press a clean cloth or bandage firmly on the wound for a few minutes until the bleeding stops.
4. **Apply an Antiseptic:** Put some antiseptic on a cotton ball and gently apply it to the wound.
5. **Cover with a Bandage:** Place a band-aid or sterile gauze over the wound and use medical tape to keep it in place.

Burns

1. **Cool the Burn:** Run cold water over the burn for about 10 minutes to cool it down. Don't use ice.
2. **Cover with Gauze:** Cover the burn with sterile gauze or a clean cloth after cooling.

3. **Elevate:** Keep it elevated to reduce swelling if it's an arm or leg burn.
4. **Don't Pop Blisters**: If you see blisters, don't pop them. They protect the burn.

Sprains and Strains
1. **Rest:** Don't use it if you hurt a joint or muscle. Rest is crucial.
2. **Ice:** Put an ice pack (a cloth with ice inside) on the area for 15-20 minutes every hour.
3. **Compression:** Use an elastic bandage to wrap the injured area gently to reduce swelling.
4. **Elevate**: Raise the injured limb to heart level, like putting a pillow under your ankle.

Bites and Stings
If you're stung by a bee, carefully scrape out the stinger with your fingernail or with a credit card.
1. **Wash with Soap:** Wash the bite or sting area with soap and water.
2. **Cold Pack:** Put a cold pack on the bite or sting to ease pain and swelling.
3. **Pain Reliever**: If it hurts, you can take a pain reliever as directed.

Allergic Reactions
1. **Stay Calm:** If you have an allergy and start to feel bad, stay calm and tell an adult.
2. **Use an EpiPen**: If you have one, use an EpiPen as instructed. Ask an adult for help.
3. **Call 911:** Ask someone to call 911 right away for more help.

Dehydration
1. **Drink Water:** When hot or sweating, drink water even if you're not thirsty.
2. **Rest in the Shade**: Find some shade to rest if you're feeling too hot.
3. **Cool Down:** Use a wet cloth on your face and neck to cool down.

Hypothermia
1. **Warm Up:** If it's cold and you're shivering, get inside a shelter or put on dry, warm clothes.

2. **Cover Up**: Use a blanket or sleeping bag to stay warm.

Basic CPR

If you know how to, begin CPR (chest compressions and rescue breaths) until help arrives. "

1. **Check for Breathing**: Tap the person and ask loudly, "Are you okay?" Check if they are breathing.
2. **Call for Help**: If they're not breathing, shout for an adult and call 911.
3. **Start CPR:** If you know how to, begin CPR (chest compressions and rescue breaths) until help arrives.

Rescue Breathing

1. **Open the Airway:** Tilt the person's head back to open their airway.
2. **Breathe for Them:** Pinch their nose and give two rescue breaths, watching their chest rise.
3. **Continue CPR:** If they're not breathing, start CPR (30 chest compressions and 2 rescue breaths).

Always try to find an adult or call 911 if someone is seriously hurt or sick. These simple steps can help you care for yourself or your friends while enjoying outdoor adventures.

Section 8: Food Finding Skills

Being capable of hunting, trapping, and gathering food in the wilderness will empower you and deepen your understanding of the natural world. These survival techniques are exciting and educational. You'll learn how to locate, catch, and harvest food from the wild, fostering resourcefulness and a deep connection with the environment. So, get ready to dive into the wilderness and discover these timeless skills that will stay with you forever.

Knowing Local Flora and Fauna

You may wonder why getting to know the plants and animals in the area where you live is incredible. It's like having a natural wonderland at your doorstep, waiting to be explored and cherished. You get to discover how everything in your environment fits together and the species dominant in the surrounding habitat. Have you ever wondered how birds find food, where frogs like to hang out, or which plants you can eat safely? These are the questions that exploring your local flora and fauna can help you answer.

With exploration, you'll discover that many plants are more than just a way of nature to add foliage to the environment. Medicine in ancient times was all made of natural elements, including medicinal plants, having tons of health benefits. The more you explore, the more you understand about foraging the right foods. Imagine picking wild berries from a hiking trail in the mountains and consuming them because you know they're perfectly safe.

But it's not just about science and survival; it's also about connecting with your community's traditions. Different places have unique ways of doing things, and by exploring your local flora and fauna, you can learn about the traditions passed down through generations. Research the plants and animals in your area to get a clear perspective of the ecosystem surrounding you. You'll be amazed to know the plants you thought were useless have health-benefiting properties when foraged and consumed correctly.

Hunting and trapping are traditional methods of obtaining wildlife for food and other resources that have been practiced for centuries. However, in the modern world, certain regulations for hunting and trapping are categorized as illegal only to conserve the ecosystem and to promote animal welfare.

These techniques have evolved over time, and today, they encompass many methods and tools. Some methods are highly advanced and use modern equipment, while others are more primitive, relying on basic tools and skills. Here, you'll explore various hunting and trapping techniques, including both modern and primitive methods:

Modern Hunting Techniques

Firearms: Firearms, such as rifles and shotguns, are the most common tools used for hunting today. They are accurate and powerful, allowing hunters to take down targets from a distance.

Bowhunting: Bowhunting involves using bows and arrows. Compound bows and crossbows are popular choices. This method requires a high skill level due to the need for accuracy and a short effective range.

Black Powder Guns: Muzzleloaders and other black powder firearms provide a more traditional hunting experience. They are slower to reload but offer a sense of history and challenge.

Crossbows: Crossbows are a modern variation of the bow and arrow, known for their accuracy and power. They are popular among hunters who appreciate the feel of traditional archery.

Scouting: Successful hunting often starts with scouting the area. Hunters look for signs of game, such as tracks, scat, and feeding areas. Understanding the terrain, vegetation, and local weather patterns is crucial.

Primitive Hunting Techniques

Snares: Snares are simple yet effective primitive tools used for trapping animals. They consist of a looped cord or wire set along animal trails or paths. When an animal passes through, the snare tightens around its body, restraining it.

Deadfalls: Deadfalls are basic trapping devices where a heavy object is propped up, and when an animal triggers it, the weight falls and crushes or traps the animal.

Cage Traps: Cage traps are more humane and catch animals without harming them. Trappers then release the captured animal at a later time.

Foot-Hold Traps: Foot-hold traps are designed to restrain an animal's leg when it steps on the trap. This allows the trapper to approach and humanely dispatch the animal.

Atlatl: The atlatl is a primitive weapon for throwing spears with more force and accuracy. It extends the hunter's arm's length, providing a mechanical advantage.

Blowgun: Blowguns are a tool used for silently hunting small game and birds. The hunter blows through the tube to propel small darts, typically poisoned, toward the target.

Remember that hunting and trapping should always be conducted ethically and with respect for wildlife and local regulations. Sustainability and responsible practices protect both the environment and the animals you target. Additionally, if you plan to engage in these activities, consider taking courses or learning from experienced individuals to ensure safe and humane practices.

Essential Fishing Skills

Wait for the fish to bite, then set the hook by quickly jerking the rod upwards when you feel a pull.[46]

Angling

You'll need a fishing rod, reel, fishing line, and various hooks, baits, and lures for angling. Choose the appropriate gear for the type of fish you're targeting. Cast your line into the water, allowing your bait or lure to float, sink, or swim at various depths. Use different casting techniques, such as overhead casting or sidearm casting, depending on your target and surroundings.

Angling requires patience. Wait for the fish to bite, then set the hook by quickly jerking the rod upwards when you feel a pull. Once you've hooked a fish, play it by reeling it in and letting it tire itself out. Use the rod to control the fish's movements and prevent it from escaping.

Setting Lines

Limblines and Juglines: These are passive fishing methods. Attach baited hooks to lines secured to floating objects like jugs or tree limbs. Submerge them in the water and check them periodically to see if you've caught any fish.

Trotlines: Trotlines are longer lines with multiple baited hooks. They are anchored in place and can be set overnight. Check them regularly to retrieve any caught fish.

Fish Traps

Hoop Nets: Hoop nets are cylindrical nets with an entrance that leads to a baited central chamber. Fish swim in but have trouble finding their way out.

Funnel Traps: These traps have a funnel-like entrance that leads to a baited chamber. Once fish enter, it's challenging for them to exit.

Spearfishing

Spearfishing requires a spear or pole with a sharp point, a mask, and a snorkel for underwater vision. A wetsuit will keep you warm and provide buoyancy. Approach fish carefully and patiently. Make a swift, accurate thrust with your spear when you get close.

Ice Fishing

Ice fishing involves fishing through a hole in the ice. You'll need an ice auger, an ice fishing rod, and warm clothing to create the hole. Popular baits for ice fishing include worms, minnows, and jigs.

Fly Fishing

Fly fishing uses a lightweight fly rod, reel, and specialized lines. The "flies" are often artificial lures made of feathers and other materials. Fly casting is a unique and graceful technique. You'll need to practice the art of casting to make the fly land gently on the water's surface.

Using Fish Finders

Modern fish finders use sonar technology to locate fish in the water. Learn how to read the display to identify fish and their depth.

Remember to check local fishing regulations and obtain any required permits or licenses. Respect catch limits and practice catch-and-release when necessary to maintain healthy fish populations. Fishing is not just a skill; it's also an opportunity to connect with nature and enjoy the great outdoors.

Tracking Skills

Look for animal footprints in the mud, sand, or snow.[47]

Animal Tracks: Look for animal footprints in the mud, sand, or snow. These prints can tell you who passed by and when.

Scat (Animal Droppings): Yes, animal poop can tell you a lot! It can show you what animals eat and their size.

Feeding Signs: Check for nibbled plants or chewed tree bark. They're like breadcrumbs leading you to possible food sources.

Prints and Trails: Follow the trail of prints to see where an animal has been and where it might be headed.

Observation Skills

Silence and Patience: Animals don't like noisy interruptions, so being quiet and patient helps you see them behaving naturally.

Binoculars and Cameras: Use binoculars or a camera to get a close-up view without scaring the animals.

Field Guides: Keep handy books to identify plants and animals in your area.

Listening: Pay attention to the sounds around you. Birds chirping or leaves rustling could reveal hidden animals.

By learning tracking and observation skills, you become a wildlife detective, discovering the secrets of nature. These skills will help you understand the natural world and make your outdoor adventures more exciting.

Tips for Hunting

Stalking Techniques

Move quietly and cautiously, keeping a low profile. Slow and deliberate movements are key to avoiding startling game animals. Take advantage of natural cover like rocks, trees, and bushes. Use them to break up your silhouette and hide from the sight of your prey. Pay attention to the wind. Keep it in your face so your scent is carried away from the animals you're pursuing. Animals rely heavily on their sense of smell. Avoid making unnecessary noise, such as stepping on dry leaves or snapping twigs. Walk softly and tread carefully.

Camouflage

Choose camouflage clothing that matches the environment you're hunting in. This helps you blend into the surroundings. Camouflage your face and hands with paint or a mask to reduce the chance of being spotted. Equip yourself with camouflage gear, including hats, gloves, and even a backpack.

Knowledge of Game Behavior

You must understand the habits and behavior of the game animals you're hunting. Study their feeding patterns, mating rituals, and preferred habitats. Hunt when your target species is most active, typically during dawn and dusk. Many animals are more active during these low-light periods. Learn to use game calls or decoys to attract or call in animals. This can be especially effective for species like waterfowl or turkeys.

Scouting

Before the hunt, scout the hunting area to identify game trails, feeding areas, and bedding sites. Place trail cameras to capture images of wildlife activity in the area. This helps you learn about game movement and timing.

Safety and Preparation

Prioritize safety by always following firearm safety rules and wearing appropriate safety gear, such as blaze orange clothing, to be visible to other hunters. Regular target practice and familiarity with your weapon will ensure accurate shooting.

Patience

Hunting requires a great deal of patience. Stay still and quiet for extended periods while waiting for your opportunity.

Ethical Considerations

Practice selective harvesting by targeting mature animals for a healthy and sustainable wildlife population. Respect wildlife by taking only ethical shots and ensuring quick, humane kills.

Remember that hunting should always be conducted ethically and under local hunting laws and regulations. A successful hunt is about bagging games, enjoying the outdoors, and respecting the natural world.

Cooking Food Safely

Safe cooking methods and proper food handling practices in the wilderness prevent foodborne illnesses and ensure a safe outdoor adventure. Here are some necessary guidelines.

Safe Cooking Methods

Cooking Over a Fire

- Use a campfire or portable camp stove for cooking. Make sure the fire is completely extinguished after use.
- Control the heat by adjusting the distance between your cookware and the flames.
- Use a meat thermometer to ensure that meat is cooked to a safe temperature (e.g., poultry to 165°F or 74°C, and ground meat to 160°F or 71°C).

Boiling Water

- Boiling water for at least one minute is one of the most effective ways to purify it, making it safe for cooking or drinking.

- Carry a reliable water purification system, such as water filters or purification tablets, if you need clarification on the water source's safety.

Use Clean Utensils

- Clean cooking utensils and cookware by scrubbing them with biodegradable soap and water. Rinse thoroughly.
- Avoid cross-contamination by using separate cutting boards and utensils for raw and cooked food.

Food Handling Practices

Hand Hygiene

- Wash your hands with soap and clean water before handling food, especially after using the restroom or handling raw meat.
- Carry hand sanitizer for situations where water and soap are unavailable.

Food Storage

- Use airtight, animal-resistant containers or bear canisters to store food. Hang food in bear bags if required in bear-prone areas.
- Keep perishable food in a cooler with ice packs to maintain safe temperatures.

Food Separation

- Keep raw meat, poultry, and seafood separate from other foods to prevent cross-contamination.
- Use sealed plastic bags or containers to prevent juices from raw meat from leaking onto other items in your backpack.

Clean Preparation Surfaces

- Use a clean, flat surface to prepare food. You can use a portable cutting board or a clean, flat rock.
- Avoid using surfaces that animals or chemicals may have contaminated.

Food Inspection

- Inspect all food for signs of spoilage or damage before consuming it.
- Discard any canned food with visible dents, leaks, or bulges.

Safe Water Sources
- Always use purified or boiled water for food preparation.
- Avoid using water from sources that may be contaminated, such as stagnant pools or water downstream from human activity.

Cooling Leftovers
- Rapidly cool leftovers to safe temperatures (below 40°F or 4°C) and store them in a cooler.
- Reheat leftovers to a high temperature before consuming.

Waste Disposal
- Dispose of food waste properly by packing it out in sealed bags. Leaving food scraps in the wilderness can attract wildlife.

Practicing safe cooking methods and food handling practices in the wilderness is crucial to prevent foodborne illnesses and maintain a healthy and enjoyable outdoor experience. Always follow Leave No Trace principles and local regulations for food storage and waste disposal in natural areas.

Section 9: Extra Bushcraft Skills and Tips

This final section provides additional skills, tips, and hacks for safe and effective bushcraft practices. They're designed to take you from being proficient in fundamental skills to becoming more advanced practitioners who can handle various scenarios and challenges in the wilderness.

Advanced Survival Skills

Signaling

Knowing distress signals and communication methods can be a lifesaver in the wilderness.[48]

Knowing distress signals and communication methods can be a lifesaver in the wilderness. If you do not have access to a radio or a phone, your hands, a piece of cloth, smoke, and other items will be useful. For example, using a whistle (a highly recommended item for your gear list for outdoor adventures) is a great way to signal distress or alert wildlife of your presence.

Whistle or Flashlight

A whistle blow is an unusual sound in the wild, and using it three times is a sure way to make others understand you need help. After each blow, pause for two seconds and then repeat. If there is anyone nearby, they'll pause and listen. Repeat the three-blow method several times to ensure you've been heard. You can use the same method using a flashlight during the night. Flash it (holding it straight ahead of you or slightly upward), turn it off, flash it again, and repeat.

Smoke

Smoke signals are a great alternative during the day. You can make a fire or use smoke from the fire you used to cook, clean, etc. You'll need a dense smoke, so add grass and other greenery. Cover the fire you aren't using for other purposes with a wet cloth when the smoke gets dense. Keep the cover on for a few seconds, then remove it to let the smoke travel upwards. After a few seconds, put the cloth back on and repeat the previous steps as needed.

Using Cloth

Because they stand out from the natural environment, brightly-colored clothing pieces can also be an alternative for creating visible signals. To signal distress, hold and wave the cloth above your head. Tie the cloth higher up around your camping area/shelter to alert wild animals. This will work in an environment where the colors are noticeable from far away, but not in a dense forest.

Shouting or Yelling

If you don't have anything for signaling, shouting or yelling at regular intervals helps, too. Apply the same principle as with other methods. Let out a loud sound, stop, and repeat as needed.

Mirrors

Tilt a mirror to catch the sunlight and aim it so the reflection goes upwards, making it easier for rescuers to see. Use this method the same way you would a whistle. Send a reflection signal for a second or two, cover it, and repeat it two more times. Wait a few seconds, then send another three signals, and repeat for as long as necessary.

Wildlife Awareness Skills

Before you embark on an outdoor adventure, learn about local wildlife and their behavior. Do you know what animals live there and where they live? Do you know what they eat and how they act when feeling threatened? If not, look it up. It will help you understand the dangers you'll face in that specific area so you can adequately prepare for them.

Besides using them as food, you'll should the wildlife. This ensures your safety and is also for the animals' well-being. Respect their space and only observe them from a safe distance. If you encounter them unexpectedly, remain calm and don't approach them. Start backing away from them and leave them room so they can do the same. If they become aggressive, don't move but start making a noise. When traveling to a new area, make noises to alert them of your presence and avoid scaring them. Beyond storing your food items securely (ideally in canisters you can hang up and away from your sleeping area), it's also a good idea to dispose of your water and food remnants safely. Leaving a trace would attract animals.

Identification Skills

Beyond identifying the tracks of animals you may want to hunt and poisonous plants to avoid foraging mishaps, you'll need other identification skills like knowing how to pick wood for different purposes. For example, softwoods like pine work better for starting a fire, whereas hardwoods are more durable and can be used for building a shelter or sustaining a fire for a long time.

Prepping and Storing Skills

Knowing how to properly prepare your food will enable you to store it safely. Understanding *how to store it* will help you conceal it from wild animals so you don't attract them. However, choosing storage space for your food can be challenging in the wilderness. Beyond hanging it up, ensure the food is kept in a dry and cool place as well. Hang your food in a sealed container in the shade (where the temperatures don't go above 90 degrees in the summer and 30 in winter). Be aware of the pests and keep them away from your food and water.

Using Glue

Packing light is essential when going on an outdoor adventure, and you might have only one of each storage item, like a water bottle. What happens if your trusty water bottle cracks? What if your tent gets damaged by the weather? These are classic situations when knowing how to use glue (a strong one, not the kind you use for school projects) will be handy.

Here are a few tips for using glue:
- Practice (under adult supervision at first) using different materials and strong adhesives.
- Put pressure on the glued item and look for cracks and fissures to determine whether the bond will hold.
- If you glue an item that's been glued before on the same place or which has an uneven surface, you'll need to sand the surface first to make the glue bond.
- Apply strong glues with their applicator or an item at hand (a piece of cloth, for example) and never with your hands.
- Clamp the two surfaces to create a stronger bond and make the process go faster.
- Read the adhesive guidelines regarding curing and drying times (the label should say when it is dry to the touch and when you can use the item safely).
- Learn what glue works best for what material (regardless of the label, some adhesives work better with some materials than others).

Alternatively, you can make glue from materials you find in the wilderness, like tree sap, resin, wax, bark, or honey. Look for sap or resin near wounded pine, fir, or spruce trees. You can also use willow and birch bark. Liquid material like sap can be used immediately after extracting it from the tree by cutting slightly into the place where you see the liquid coming out from a wound. If you're using hard material like resin or bark, chop it up into tiny pieces, mix it with water (1 part plant material, 2 parts water), bring to a boil in a pot, and cook it over a slow fire until it thickens (about 30 minutes).

Additional Bushcraft Tips

Keeping Yourself Entertained

If you're used to entertaining yourself with gadgets or hanging out with friends in a busy urban area, you'll be surprised how bored you'll get in the wilderness. It's quiet, and if you're out with a larger group, all tasks will be done in no time, so you'll have plenty of time on your hands. The good news is that keeping yourself entertained is a skill you can learn through *practice*. Moreover, the bigger your group is, the greater the chances that someone will devise a plan for engaging everyone and making your adventure a fun experience. Think about what you could do that doesn't involve electronics or making loud noises. Games that don't require much gear and lookout schedules (for animals and plants you've previously read about) are great options.

Make Practice Fun

Everything is easier to learn if you make practicing it fun. For example, you can turn the practice of identifying stones into something more, like a rock-throwing contest. When looking for firewood, you could list other purposes for what you've gathered (like making a shelter, using a sharp stick for spearing fish, etc.)

Work on Your Awareness

Moving with stealth, patience, and situation awareness are two crucial skills you'll need in the wilderness. On the one hand, you'll need to move in such a way as to make as little noise as possible. On the other hand, you must know when to stop and listen out for signs of wildlife. It will also teach you how to wait patiently and in silence. You can practice this by listening to how others move through the house or outdoors when no other noises are around.

Get Used to Sleeping in Unusual Places

If you're used to sleeping in a dark room in a comfortable bed, out in nature, every little sound or sign of discomfort will wake you up. You can make your shelter as comfortable as possible by using the right materials - but you'll still need to learn how to sleep with nature's sounds and being a little uncomfortable (like if you're sleeping area is a bit warmer than usual or when you don't have as much room as you're used to having in your bed). Sleeping better will help you be more alert during the day to avoid mistakes and injuries.

Practice Often

Everyone learns at different speeds based on their interests, supplies, abilities, and opportunities. This is entirely normal. Don't be discouraged if you can't master a skill immediately. Everyone makes mistakes when learning something. Practice makes perfect, and some skills take longer to learn than others. Start with the basics and practice them as often as possible. Only move on to advanced skills when you're confident with the basics. Practicing repeatedly will also enable you to learn from your mistakes much sooner.

Practice even those bushcraft skills you are good at so you won't get out of practice. Some skills are easier to remember, while others aren't. If you don't practice the skills you've already mastered, you could fail to get them right in an emergency situation or when you're feeling tired after a long day spent outdoors.

Learn to Work with Others

While exploring nature with a group can be fun, there will be times when not everyone will get along. You might disagree on how something should be done. However, for everyone's safety, you must learn how to work with others even if you don't get along with them or disagree with their opinion. Sometimes you just have to compromise.

Another issue that might arise is the feeling that not everyone does their share of the workload. For example, you may get upset because one person refused to clean up while others went for supplies and cooked. Instead of getting angry, ask them why they didn't clean up and listen to their side regardless of your feelings. After listening to them, explain why you think their behavior is unfair and try to reach a compromise.

You should also listen to what others say when you disagree on doing something. Listening to them will help you understand why they want to do it the way they do, and you'll be able to decide whether you disagree. Showing you care about other people's opinions is necessary for good teamwork. It builds camaraderie and ensures everyone will know to count on others to survive and thrive in the wild.

Practice Relaxing

While staying alert is needed many times in the wilderness, being in this state will make you anxious and stressed. It will cause you to sleep poorly and overreact to every little noise or sight that appears suddenly. Sometimes, you need to relax and let others (and your gear and protective measures) keep you safe.

Think before You Act

The wilderness can be unpredictable, but with good preparation, you can predict and learn what to do in every circumstance. If you find yourself in a situation where you don't know what will happen next, take a moment to think. Your action can make a difference in staying safe or walking into a dangerous situation like encountering wild animals or finding yourself in a terrain full of hidden perils. Think about where you are and what dangers could lie ahead in your current location. In the beginning, this will be a challenging skill to master, but it will become much easier with practice.

Thank You Message

Thank you for choosing and reading this book. By the end of the book, you've become richer with a broad range of skills and knowledge about how to survive in the wild. You've learned what gear you need for bushcraft, how to secure knots, build a shelter and a fire, find water and food resources, and what to do if someone gets hurt or ill. Spending time in nature can be a scary prospect. However, now that you have acquired all these skills, you have nothing to fear anymore because you will know what to do in every situation. Although it's always advisable to explore the outdoors in the company of adults, having some bushcraft tricks up your sleeves will help you become more independent during your adventures.

Now, it is time to put your knowledge into practice as you continue learning about bushcraft. Remember, this is a complex set of skills that takes time, dedication, and patience to master. Besides, the more bushcraft talents you master, the higher your chances of survival should you find yourself without help in the wilderness.

You can help organize your next adventure and showcase your newly acquired skills only on your journey. Taking the initiative and actively keeping yourself and others safe in your outdoor explorations will further empower you with much-needed practical experience. As you do, you can use this book as a stepping stone and a reference for your future learning about bushcraft and wilderness survival.

Practicing what you learned from this book will make you more confident in your practical outdoor skills. As you apply these talents, you'll see just how many adventures the great outdoors holds. At times, it will teach you how to be more independent and think outside the box, while in other circumstances, it will give you a chance to admire the natural beauties you can only see in the wilderness. Once again, thank you, and congratulations on completing this book and embarking on your very first bushcraft journey.

Part 2: Gardening for Kids

Growing Fruits, Vegetables, and Green Thumbs in Young Gardeners

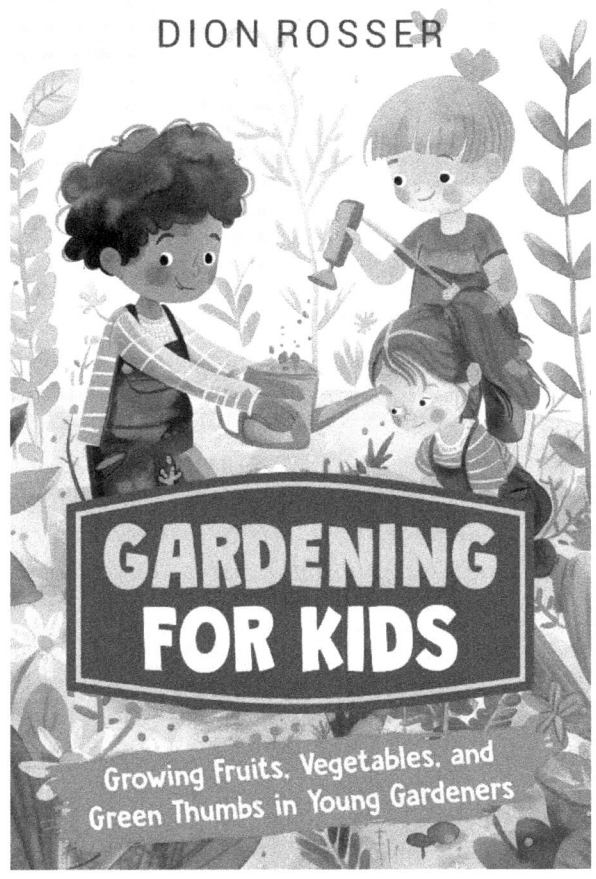

Introduction Letter to Parents

Dear Parents,

In today's fast-paced society, where screens dominate children's attention, it has become increasingly important to reconnect with nature and instill a love for the outdoors. Gardening provides the perfect opportunity to do just that. Not only does it offer children a chance to grow beautiful plants, but it also teaches them essential life skills and values. Scattered throughout the pages of this book is a multitude of benefits that gardening brings to the young ones. From encouraging responsibility and patience to developing a deep appreciation for the environment, gardening is a holistic learning experience that goes far beyond soil and seeds.

As parents and guardians, your active involvement and support in your children's gardening experience cannot be overstated. Participating alongside them creates a safe space for exploration, delightful discoveries, and shared memories. The garden becomes a canvas for quality time, where bonds are strengthened, and conversations flow freely.

Gardening is much more than the physical act of planting and tending to plants. It is an opportunity for deep personal growth. As you walk this journey with your children, you have the unique opportunity to motivate their curiosity by going on a quest for knowledge yourself. Become immersed in the fascinating world of plants, insects, and ecological concepts as a family. Let their questions take you on a path of exploration and research as you unravel the wonders of nature side by side. Encourage your children to express themselves through their garden projects. Let them choose their favorite plants, design their own small sections, and even make DIY garden decorations. By allowing their imagination to run free and granting them a sense of ownership, you give them the power to take pride in their creations and appreciate the beauty and significance hidden in each experience. And just like that, you will have sown the seeds of love for nature and reap the bountiful fruits of a patient, responsible, and creative child – and a shared gardening adventure.

Introduction Letter to Children

Hey there, kids!

Have you ever held a tiny seed in your hand? It's so small and simple. But within that humble shell lies the potential for greatness: the power to create life and beauty. With your tender care and protection, you will witness the miracle of that seed sprouting, stretching its green arms toward the sun, and transforming into the most precious plant. That is gardening. It is a front-row seat to the most captivating show on Earth.

But gardening is not just about witnessing miracles; it's about being a magician yourself. You'll learn the secrets of turning dry, lifeless soil into a fertile playground where plants live and bloom in peace. You'll discover the perfect balance of sun, water, and nutrients that will make your plants grow tall and proud. As you explore this delicate world as a gardener, nature will reward you with surprises at every turn: a hidden ladybug, a beautiful butterfly, or the refreshing smell of a blooming flower.

The garden is the most interesting classroom you'll ever walk into, where you'll soak up knowledge faster than the speed of a sprouting seed. Each plant you nurture will teach you things you never knew about biology, ecology, and how all living things are connected somehow. You'll become a detective, investigating the mysteries of pests and diseases, and a master problem-solver, finding the smartest ways to protect your green friends. Gardening is an adventure that promises laughter, surprises, and unforgettable moments. There are few experiences like the thrill of harvesting your own vegetables and biting into a juicy berry that you have grown with your own two hands. And when your friends come over, your garden will be the ultimate playground: a place of imagination and pure fun.

The pages of this book offer you all the inspiration, tips, and secrets you need. It's a portal to a world where plants whisper their wisdom, where you'll find answers to your burning questions, and where imagination takes root and grows alongside your plants. This book will be your trusted partner as you begin your life as a gardener. It will encourage you to dream big. It will guide you every step of the way, and before you know it, you will have gone from a curious beginner to a skilled gardener simply *because you can.*

Chapter 1: Garden Basics

Garden basics are the building blocks of every garden. Just as a house needs a strong base to stand on, a garden needs a few important things to help it grow into something amazing. As a newbie gardener, you'll need all the basic ideas to start your garden, but gardening isn't just about facts and science. It's also about having fun and enjoying yourself!

A garden can bring so much joy to your life. Imagine watching a tiny seed sprout into a beautiful flower or a delicious vegetable you can eat. This experience connects you with nature. It teaches you to be patient and take care of things and gives you a peaceful place to relax. So, put on your gardening gloves and cool sun hat, and prepare to create the best garden in your neighborhood!

Finding Your Garden Location

When it comes to finding the perfect spot for your garden, there are a few things to keep in mind so that your plants come out strong and healthy.

First, sunlight. You need the sun to feel warm and full of energy, right? Plants need sunlight to make their food and grow big and strong. So, look for a place in your yard where the sun shines for at least six hours daily. That way, your plants will have plenty of sunshine to soak up.

Shade is nice on a hot day, but too much shade can make it hard for plants to get the sunlight they need. So, avoid spots under big, tall trees or buildings that block out a lot of sunlight. Plants like to bask in the warm sunbeams, too.

Look for a place in your yard that gets a lot of sun.[49]

Next, check the soil. Think of soil as the cozy blanket that your plants snuggle into. You want the soil to be soft, crumbly, and easy for the plant roots to wiggle through. Take a look at the ground in your garden spot. If it's hard or rocky, you can make it better by adding some special stuff called compost or soil mix. It gives your plants a comfortable place to call home. Water is important too, just like it is for you. Plants need water to drink and stay hydrated. So, having a water source nearby, like a hose or a rain barrel, is a good idea. That way, you can easily give your plants a nice drink whenever they need it.

Finally, choose a garden spot that's easy for you to get to. You'll want to visit your garden as much as possible to take care of your plants, water them, and pick some vegetables or pretty flowers. So, pick a spot that's close to your house. That way, you can quickly hop, skip, and jump to your garden whenever you want.

How to Design Your Garden

Designing a garden makes you an artist, creating a beautiful masterpiece with plants and colors. Of course, there are a few things to think about, but the most important thing is to let your imagination run wild and be creative. Nonetheless, here are a few things to think about when designing the perfect garden:

- **Balance and Symmetry:** In your garden, you want to create balance by having tall plants or things on one side and shorter ones on the other. It's like having a big friend on one side of the seesaw and a smaller one on the other. This helps your garden look even and organized. Symmetry, however, means having things that look the same on both sides of your garden, like when you fold a piece of paper in half and both sides match. You can create symmetry by having two pretty flower beds or two pots with colorful flowers that look alike on both sides.
- **Size:** Next, consider size and proportion. See your garden as a big puzzle where all the pieces fit together just right. How much space do you have in your garden? Is it a big backyard or a small space? Your answer will help you decide how many plants and decorations you can fit in. Now, think about the size of the plants and objects you want to include. Some plants can grow really tall, like a giant sunflower, while others stay small and cute, like a tiny daisy. When you're drawing a picture, and you want everything to look right, you are applying the rules of *size and proportion*. You should do the same thing to your garden. For example, if you have a small garden, it might look funny if you put a huge tree in the middle, but if you have a big garden, a tall tree could be just right.
- **Color and Texture:** For color, you can choose flowers and plants in all different colors to make it look pretty. Imagine having red, yellow, blue, and purple flowers all together. It's an insane explosion of colors. You can even have flowers that change colors as the seasons go by, so your garden always looks new and exciting. Now, texture is all about how things feel when you touch them. Plants can have different textures in the same way that some toys are smooth and others are bumpy. Some leaves are soft and smooth, while others are rough or fuzzy. You can choose plants with different textures to make your garden fun to touch, not just fun to look at

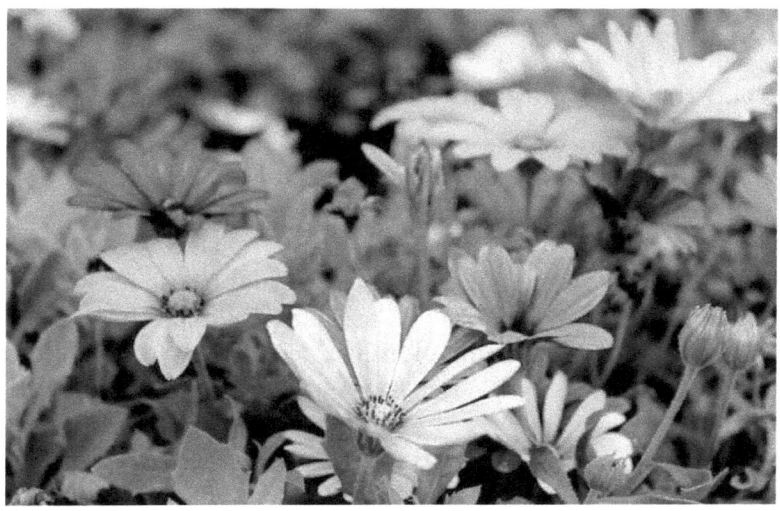

You can choose different colored plants to make your garden look pretty.[50]

- **Decorations**: Feel free to add some pathways and cool decorations or toys. You can make paths that lead to different places in your garden, like secret hideouts or unique decorations. Use tiny stones, bricks, or even pebbles to make your paths. And don't forget the decorations, like a pretty statue, a shiny fountain, or a colorful bench. These things make your garden totally cool!

Fertilizing

Fertilizing is the act of giving food to plants so they can stay healthy and grow properly. Plants need nutrients like *nitrogen, phosphorus, and potassium* to survive and be happy. These nutrients help them make strong stems, beautiful leaves, and colorful flowers. But sometimes, the soil in a garden doesn't have enough of these nutrients, and that's when fertilizing comes in.

Fertilizers are *plant foods*. They are made with all the important nutrients that plants need. When you sprinkle or spread the fertilizer in the soil around the plants, they can suck it down into their roots. By adding fertilizers, you ensure that your plants have all the nutrients they need to be the best plants they can be.

Fertilizing also gives plants a shield against problems like diseases and pests. When plants get the right nutrients, they become strong and healthy. The same happens when you eat good food; you can fight germs better and not fall sick. Well-fed plants do it, too; they can protect themselves from nasty diseases and dangerous pests that can hurt them. So, by giving your plants the special plant food (fertilizer) they need, you're giving them the power to stay healthy and safe for as long as they live.

But remember, you have to be careful with fertilizers. Using too much can actually cause problems for your plants. It's like eating too much candy—it might taste good, but it's not good for your body. Too much fertilizer can hurt the roots of plants. So, you need to use the right amount and follow the instructions. You can ask an adult to help you with this. They can guide you on how much fertilizer to use and when. They can be your gardening buddy to make sure you're doing everything correctly.

Watering

Plants need water to quench their thirst and keep their stems happy, but you must be careful and water them correctly. When you water plants, it's best to pour the water at the base of the plant, near the roots. That's where the roots drink the water and send it to all parts of the plant. Instead of just splashing water on the leaves all the time, you'll be giving them a refreshing drink right where they need it the most. Every good gardener knows to avoid watering the leaves or flowers too much because it can make them wet for too long. Wet leaves and flowers can get sick and cause problems. You wouldn't want to stay wet for a long time, would you? You might catch a cold or get sick, too. For that reason, you should aim for the base of the plants as much as you can.

Plants need water to survive.[51]

Watering is important, but you must also find the right balance. You don't want to overwater or underwater your plants. Overwatering means giving them too much water, like pouring a whole bucket when they only need a little sip. Too much water can drown the roots and make the plant sick. This doesn't happen to just plants; if you drink too much water, you might feel sick and uncomfortable.

On the other hand, underwatering means not giving enough water to your plants, like when you're really thirsty and only get a tiny sip. If plants don't get enough water, they can become weak and wilted. They might not grow well, make pretty flowers, or produce good fruits.

So, how do you know when to water your plants? You can check the soil by sticking your finger about an inch deep into it. If it feels dry, it's time to water it, but you can wait a little longer if it feels wet. Each plant has different needs, so it's necessary to learn about the specific needs of the plants in your garden. Always remember watering plants is necessary, but you must do it right. Water at the base of the plants, avoid overwatering or underwatering – and check the soil so you know when your plants are thirsty!

Choosing Plants for Your Garden: All You Need to Know

1. **Space:** When choosing plants for your garden, consider how much space they need to grow. Some plants, like sunflowers, can grow really tall and need lots of room to spread their leaves. Other plants, like some herbs, stay small and can be grown in containers or small gardens. So, do your best to pick plants that fit nicely in your garden space.

2. **Care:** In the same way that we don't all have the same needs, plants have different needs, too. Some plants love to soak up the sun all day, while others prefer a bit of shade to keep them cool. Some plants need lots of water, while others are okay with less. For your sake and the sake of your garden, it's better to choose plants that match the conditions in your garden and are easy for you to take care of. That way, you and your plants have a relationship that you both enjoy.

3. **Fun Factor:** Your garden should definitely be super fun and exciting. You can choose plants that are unique and interesting.

Look for flowers that attract butterflies with their bright colors and sweet smells. You can also find plants with cool shapes and textures, like fuzzy leaves or spiky flowers. All these plants will make your garden almost magical and the best one you've ever seen.

Chapter 2: Tools You'll Need

Garden tools can be the difference between a happy, healthy garden and a messy, untamed jungle. In gardening, tools are the instruments that help people take care of plants and make gardening easier and less like work. They save you time and energy by giving you faster ways to dig, prune, water, and maintain your garden. Without the right tools, tasks that should be fun can quickly become unending and frustrating. For example, using a shovel or trowel helps you dig holes faster than using just your hands. A watering can helps you water plants more evenly and without wasting water. Pruning shears make it quick and easy to trim plants so they stay healthy, and the other tools help you do different tasks in the garden without getting tired or messy. So, just like tools help you with different things at school or at home, gardening tools help you take care of plants and make gardening fun and easy.

Importance of Garden Tools

Garden tools can improve your gardening experience.[52]

Using the right garden tools will improve your garden and your gardening experience. Here's how:

1. **Get Things Done Faster**: Garden tools help you finish gardening tasks more quickly. They make digging, cutting, and taking out weeds easier and faster.

2. **Do Things Just Right**: Each garden tool is made for a specific job. They help you do things exactly the way you want. For example, pruning shears helps you cut branches neatly, and a trowel helps you make perfect little holes for planting.
3. **Get More Work Done:** When you use garden tools, you can do more work in less time. Tools like wheelbarrows, garden carts, and rakes help you move things like soil, leaves, and other stuff faster so you can finish your tasks quickly.
4. **Stay Safe and Protected**: Garden tools keep you safe while you work in the garden. Gloves, knee pads, and goggles protect you from thorns, sharp things, and dirt that can hurt you.
5. **Do Lots of Different Things:** Garden tools can do many different jobs. For example, a garden knife can dig, cut, and pull out weeds, while a garden fork helps loosen soil and move plants.
6. **Last a Long Time**: Good garden tools are strong and last a long time. If you care for them, they will keep working well for a while, so you won't have to buy new ones for years.
7. **Easy to Use:** Garden tools are made to be easy for everyone to use. They have comfortable handles and are not too heavy, so you can use them without getting tired or hurting yourself.
8. **Stay Organized:** Having garden tools helps you stay organized. You can keep them in one place; when you need them, they're ready to go. This way, you don't waste time looking for them.

Categories of Garden tools

- **Digging Tools**

Sometimes, you need to dig holes in the ground to plant seeds or move plants when gardening. There are special tools that can help you with this. One tool looks like a big scoop with a long handle. It's great for digging deep holes in the soil. Another tool is like a smaller scoop that fits in your hand. It's lighter and easier to use for digging smaller holes. There's also a tool that has a flat, square-shaped blade. It helps you dig and move soil when you need to make a trench or turn over the soil. And finally, there's a tool with pointy prongs. It's good for loosening the soil and breaking up clumps. These special tools make it easier for you to dig in the garden. Instead of your hands, use these tools to dig quickly and get the job done faster.

- **Cutting and Pruning Tools**

When caring for your plants, you will need to trim or cut away some parts to help them grow better. Cutting and pruning tools are simply scissors for plants. They help you remove extra branches or leaves that may be getting too big or are not healthy anymore. Just as you get haircuts to keep your hair healthy and neat, plants sometimes need a little trim, too!

- **Watering Tools**

Plants can't do without water because they need it to grow and stay healthy. You use tools to help give your plants the right amount of water. These tools help you gently pour water on the plants to ensure you give them the right amount, not too much or too little. They make it easier to water plants. You can water them evenly and ensure each plant gets the water it needs.

- **Planting Tools**

You use planting tools to plant new seeds or move plants to a different spot. Planting tools make putting the seeds or plants into the ground easier. They are the helpers that create little holes in the soil. You can then gently place the seeds or plants into these holes. Planting tools make planting so much easier; you have no idea! You can plant your favorite flowers, vegetables, or herbs without getting your hands all dirty.

- **Maintenance Tools**

Once in a while, your garden needs some tender, loving care, too. Maintenance tools keep your garden clean and healthy. One thing you will be doing as maintenance is removing the weeds. Weeds are unwanted plants that grow where you don't want them to. You can use these tools to pull them out of the ground so they don't take nutrients away from your plants.

Another thing you will be doing is tidying up your plants. Sometimes, they grow too big or have parts that are not healthy. You can use some tools to trim or cut away these extra parts. And remember to clean up fallen leaves or other messes in your garden. Use tools to gather the leaves and keep your garden neat. When you use maintenance tools, you take good care of your garden and ensure your plants have everything they need to look good and feel good. It is your way of showing your love and responsibility.

Basic Tools You'll Need

1. **Shovel:** A shovel is a tool with a long handle and a scoop-shaped blade at the end. It comes in many different sizes. It is used to dig holes in the ground. You can use a shovel to dig a hole for planting seeds or to transplant plants from one place to another.
2. **Watering Can:** A watering can is a special container with a spout and a handle. It is used to water plants. Fill the watering can with water and gently pour the water around the base of your plants. This helps them stay hydrated and healthy.

A watering can is used to water plants. [53]

3. **Trowel:** A trowel is a small, handheld tool with a pointed blade. It is used to dig small holes when planting tiny flowers or herbs. Hold the handle of the trowel and push it into the soil to make a hole. Then, place your plant or seedling into the hole and cover it with soil.
4. **Gloves:** Gloves are protective covers for your hands. They keep your hands safe and clean while you work in the garden. Wear gloves to protect your hands from thorns, prickly plants, or dirt. They also prevent any scratches or cuts.
5. **Pruning Shears**: Pruning shears are scissors for plants. They trim or cut branches, leaves, or flowers from plants. When using pruning shears, be careful to only cut the parts of the plant that you

need to. This will keep your plants looking good and encourage new growth.
6. **Rake:** A rake is a tool with a long handle and a row of teeth or prongs. It gathers leaves, grass, or other garden rubbish into piles. Hold the rake handle and slide it across the soil to gently gather the leaves or grass on the ground.

As easy as garden tools are to use, it is always safer to ask an adult for help and guidance. They can show you how to use the tools safely and teach you more about caring for plants.

Choosing the Best Tools for Your Age

When selecting tools for gardening, you should find ones that are just right for your age and size. Some tools are specially made in smaller sizes and designed for children like you. These tools are easier to hold and use because they are made with your needs in mind. Here are a few things to remember when you go shopping for tools:

1. **Size:** Look for tools that are smaller and lighter. They should fit well in your hands and be easy to hold. This way, you can use them comfortably without straining your muscles.
2. **Safety:** Safety is always important. Make sure the tools you choose have smooth edges and aren't too sharp. You want to avoid any accidents or cuts while working in the garden.
3. **Durability:** Find strong and durable tools; these will last a long time, and you can continue using them for many gardening adventures.
4. **Fun Designs**: Some gardening tools come in fun colors or with cool patterns. Choosing tools that you find visually interesting can make you excited to work in your garden.

Safety Rules

Nobody likes rules, but safety rules are not meant to hold you back or tell you what to do. They are there to keep you safe so that you are comfortable and have the best experience doing whatever you are doing. There are safety rules for everything, and that includes gardening and the use of garden tools. Here are the most important ones you should know:

- **Ask for Adult Supervision**: Always have an adult with you when using garden tools, at least at first. They can guide you and make sure you're using the tools safely.

- **Wear Safety Gear:** Wear gardening gloves to protect your hands from prickly plants and germs. Depending on the task, you might also need safety goggles to protect your eyes.
- **Use Tools for Their Intended Purpose**: Each tool has a specific job. Use the tools only for what they're meant to do. For example, don't use a trowel as a toy or a rake as a pretend sword. You might hurt yourself or, even worse, someone else.
- **Handle Tools with Care:** Treat your tools gently and with respect. Avoid swinging them around or playing rough games with them. Remember, they are not toys.
- **Watch Your Fingers**: Keep your fingers away from the sharp parts of the tools, like blades or prongs. Always pay attention to where they are while using the tools to avoid accidents.
- **Store Tools Properly:** When you have finished gardening for the day, put them away in a safe place. Store them where they won't be a tripping hazard or where younger children can't reach them.
- **Clean up After Yourself:** After using the tools, clean them and put them away neatly. This will keep the tools in good condition and make them last longer.
- **Be Aware of Your Surroundings:** Look around and make sure there are no obstacles or people nearby that you might accidentally hit with the tools. Give yourself plenty of space to work safely.

How to Clean and Care for Your Garden Tools

- **Step One: Gather Your Cleaning Supplies**: Get a bucket of warm, soapy water and a clean cloth or sponge.
- **Step Two: Remove Dirt and Debris:** Use a cloth or sponge to wipe off any dirt, mud, or plant residue from your tools. Make sure to clean both the blades and handles of your tools.
- **Step Three: Rinse with Water:** After removing the dirt, rinse your tools with clean water to wash away any remaining soap and dirt.

- **Step Four: Disinfect Your Tools**: To prevent the spread of diseases between plants, you should disinfect your tools. You can do this by using a solution of one part bleach to nine parts water. Get an adult for this. Dip a clean cloth or sponge into the solution and wipe down the blades and handles of your tools. Let them sit for a few minutes.
- **Step Five: Rinse and Dry**: After disinfecting, rinse your tools with clean water again to remove any leftover bleach. Then, use a dry cloth or towel to thoroughly dry your tools. Water can cause tools to rust, so drying them is important.
- **Step Six: Store in a Dry Place**: Once your tools are clean and dry, store them in a dry place. This prevents rust and keeps them in good condition for future use.
- **Step Seven: Clean Your Cleaning Supplies**: After cleaning your tools, remember to clean your bucket, cloth, or sponge. Rinse them thoroughly and let them dry before putting them away.

By cleaning and caring for your tools after each use, you're keeping them in good shape and preventing the spread of diseases that can harm your plants. It's a great way to take care of your tools and your garden at the same time.

Chapter 3: Fruits and Vegetables

You can enjoy fresh and tasty food all year round when you grow your own fruit and vegetables. You get to pick them when they are perfectly ripe and full of flavor, and that's way better than buying them from the store, where they might not be as fresh all the time. Eating fruit and vegetables is really good for your health. When you grow your own, you can choose to use natural ways to care for them. For example, you can use friendly bugs to eat the bad bugs or using compost instead of chemicals, keeping your harvest healthier and safer.

Growing your own food can also save you money. While you might need to spend a little bit of money to get started with seeds and tools, in the long run, it's much cheaper than buying fresh fruits and vegetables from the store. And the more you grow, the more you can save by storing or preserving them for later. When you grow your own food, you're also helping the environment. By not relying on food that has to travel long distances, you're doing your part to reduce pollution from transportation. You can also choose to use organic growing methods, which means no chemicals that can hurt the earth.

Gardening is a great way to get outside and stay active, but watching your plants grow and seeing them produce fruits is the icing on the cake. It's a project you have taken great care of, and it feels amazing when you see the results. It's something to be proud of and makes you feel really good about yourself. Growing your own food is also a chance to learn and discover new things. You get to learn how plants grow, how to care for them, and the bugs and animals that help them grow. It's your own mini-science experiment right in your backyard.

And finally, when you grow your own food, it can bring people together. You get to share what you grow with your friends, family, and neighbors. It's a great way to connect with others and have fun together. So, growing fruits and vegetables is not only exciting and rewarding, but it also helps you eat more healthily, save money, take care of the environment, learn new things, and make the best memories.

Soil Preparation

Preparing the soil is key to growing the sweetest and healthiest fruits and vegetables. First, understand that plants get their food from the soil. In the same way you need healthy food to grow strong as a human, plants need nutritious soil to grow big and tasty. So, soil preparation can translate to making the best meal for your plants.

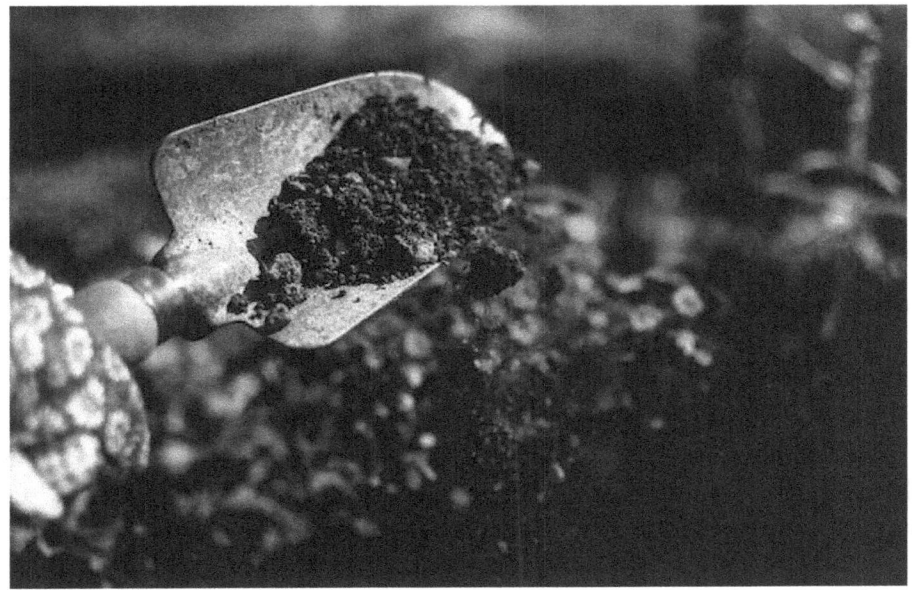

Soil preparation is the key to growing the sweetest and healthiest fruits and vegetables.[54]

You start by clearing the area where you want to grow your plants. You remove any weeds or grass that might be there. This way, your plants have space to grow without any competition. Next, you need to loosen up the soil. You use tools like shovels or rakes to gently break up the soil. This helps the roots of the plants move around easily in the soil and reach the nutrients they need. After that, you add compost or natural fertilizers to the soil. Compost is made from fruit and vegetable scraps, leaves, and other organic materials. It's a special treat just for your soil. These natural fertilizers have lots of nutrients that plants love. They make the soil healthy and give your plants the energy they need to do their best.

Once you've added the compost, you need to mix it into the soil. Be gentle and take your time because you want the nutrients to spread evenly so that all your plants can get their fair share. Look at it like stirring a pot of soup to make sure all the ingredients blend together nicely. Now, your soil is ready for planting. You can put your seeds or tiny plants into the soil, cover them gently with some more soil, and give them a little drink of water. This helps them feel cozy and safe as they start to grow.

Why is all this soil preparation important? Well, you are creating a perfect home for your plants. You're giving them a good start in life and the best chance to produce the tastiest fruit and vegetables you've ever had. Gardening is a mission, and soil preparation is an important part of that mission. You owe it to your plants to get your hands dirty, mix in some compost, and make the soil fluffy and comfortable for them.

Soil Testing and Amending

Soil testing is a check-up for the soil. It helps you understand what the soil is like and what extra things it might need to make your plants happy. To do a soil test, you take a small soil sample and send it to a special lab. The scientists in the lab will test the soil to see what nutrients it has and if anything is missing. You can also buy soil testing kits. Once you get the soil test results, you can know if your soil needs any adjustments. Sometimes, the soil might have less nutrients than your plants need; if that is the case, you can amend it.

Amending means adding things to the soil to make it better. You can add compost, manure, or organic fertilizers to prepare the soil for planting. Adding compost to your garden gives the plants more nutrients to eat and helps the soil hold onto water like a sponge. Manure might sound a little funny, but it's actually poop from animals, particularly cows, chickens, or horses. But don't worry; it's clean and safe for your plants. It contains the necessary things to grow, like nitrogen, phosphorus, and potassium. Think vitamin shake, but ONLY for plants.

Planting: The Process

Planting seeds, seedlings, or young plants is an exciting part of growing fruits and vegetables. You'll need some tips to help you with this:

- **Start by Preparing the Soil:** Clear the area where you want to plant your seeds or seedlings. Remove any weeds or grass to give your plants space to grow.
- **Dig a Hole:** Use a small shovel or your hands to dig a hole in the soil. The hole should be deep enough for the roots of your plants to fit comfortably.
- **Planting Seeds:** If you're planting seeds, follow the instructions on the seed packet. Some seeds need to be planted deeper, while others should be closer to the surface. Drop the seeds into the hole and cover them with a thin layer of soil. Gently pat the soil down to make sure the seeds are snug and secure.
- **Planting Seedlings or Young Plants:** If you're planting seedlings or young plants, gently remove them from their pots or containers. Place the root ball (the clump of soil around the roots) into the hole you have dug, and make sure the plant stands up straight. Then, cover the roots with soil, gently patting it down around the base of the plant.
- **Proper Planting Depth:** Seeds or seedlings do better if planted correctly. Too deep, and they might struggle to reach the surface. Too shallow, and they may not get enough support. The seed packet or instructions that come with seedlings usually tell you how deep to plant them. Follow those guidelines to make sure you're doing it right.
- **Spacing Your Plants:** Each plant needs space to spread its roots. If plants are too close together, they'll start fighting for sunlight, water, and food. The seed packet or instructions should inform you of how much space each plant needs. Leave enough room between plants so that they have space to grow without crowding each other or fighting all the time.
- **Water Your Plants:** After planting, give your seeds, seedlings, or young plants a nice drink of water. This helps them settle into their new home and gives them the moisture they need to start their lives.

Proper Watering Practices

- Give your plants a drink about one knuckle deep when the soil feels dry.
- Pour the water close to the bottom of the plant, where the roots are.
- Use a watering can with a spout or a gentle hose to water your plants.
- Water your plants in the morning or evening when it's not too hot outside.
- Don't give your plants too much water. Just make the soil feel damp, like a sponge wrung out, but not soaking wet like a puddle.
- Watch out for signs that your plants are thirsty, for example, leaves that look droopy or soil that feels really dry.
- If you have delicate plants, be extra careful when you water them. Use a mist or spray bottle to moisten the soil.
- Before you water your plants, check the weather forecast. If rain is on the way, you might not need to water them as much. You can adjust how often you water based on what the weather is doing.

Fruits

Apples

- **Edible Parts**: Apples have a tasty and crunchy part that you can eat. It's the juicy part around the core in the middle.
- **Seeds:** Apples have tiny seeds inside the middle part, the core.
- **Proper Care:** To grow apple trees, find a sunny spot with soil that drains water well. Give them enough water, and trim them regularly.

Things to Remember

1. Apple trees need help from other apple trees to make lots of fruits. So, it's a good idea to plant two different kinds of apple trees close to each other.

2. Sometimes, apple trees grow too many apples, so it's better to take some fruit off the tree. That way, the ones that are left will be bigger and sweeter.

Raspberries
- **Edible Parts:** The juicy berries that grow on prickly branches.
- **Seeds:** Raspberries have tiny seeds hiding inside the berry.
- **Proper Care:** Raspberry plants prefer to be placed somewhere sunny in soil that lets water drain away. Help the branches climb by giving them something to hold onto, and make sure to give them water regularly.

Things to Remember
1. Trim the old branches of raspberry plants to make room for new ones to grow.
2. Pick raspberries when they are fully ripe and come easily off the plant.

Blueberry

Blueberries are small and round.[55]

- **Edible Parts:** The small, round berries that taste sweet and tangy.
- **Seeds:** Inside the berry, you can find tiny seeds.
- **Proper Care:** For blueberry plants, find a place with slightly acidic soil that lets water flow away. They like to be in the sun, but some shade is okay, too. Make sure to give them water regularly so the soil stays damp.

Things to Remember
1. Blueberries like acidic soil, so you can add peat moss or pine needles to make the soil more acidic.
2. During the season when the plants aren't growing much, trim off the old branches to make room for new ones to grow.

Watermelon
- **Edible Parts:** The juicy and sweet flesh inside their big, green outer shell.
- **Seeds:** Watermelons have a lot of seeds inside.
- **Proper Care**: Watermelon plants like a lot of sun and soil that doesn't soak up too much water. Give them lots of water, though, especially when it's hot and dry.

Things to Remember
1. Watermelon plants like to spread out, so make sure they have lots of space to grow.
2. Pick the watermelon when the bottom part changes from light green to creamy yellow.

Tomato
- **Edible Parts:** The round, juicy parts that come in red or yellow colors.
- **Seeds:** Inside the tomato, you can find lots of tiny seeds.
- **Proper Care:** Tomato plants love the sun and light soil with good drainage. Give them water regularly so the soil is always a little wet.

Things to Remember
1. Tomato plants are naturally climbing plants, so they need something to lean on and support them, like sticks or cages, to stay upright as they grow.
2. Take away extra branches called suckers to help the plant use its energy for making fruits.

Vegetables

Carrot

- **Edible Parts:** Carrots have long, crunchy orange roots that you can eat.
- **Seeds:** To grow carrots, you will need to buy carrot seeds.
- **Proper Care:** When you want to grow carrot plants, find loose and sandy soil. Water them regularly so the soil stays damp.

Things to Remember

1. To help your carrots, remove some of the seedlings to give each carrot enough space.
2. Putting a layer of mulch around the plants can keep the soil cool and save water.

Pumpkin

Pumpkin.[56]

- **Edible Parts:** The sweet, orange flesh inside the tough outer shell.
- **Seeds:** Inside the pumpkin, you can find big seeds.
- **Proper Care:** Pumpkins need lots of space to spread out, so your garden needs to be big enough. Remember to water them really well.

Things to Remember
1. Pumpkin plants like to have lots of room, so make sure they have plenty of space to grow big.
2. Pick the pumpkins when fully ripe and the outside is hard.

Build a Specialty Garden

A specialty garden is a rare kind of garden that focuses on growing specific types of plants or creating a unique theme. It's a garden that is all about one particular thing that you really like. Take a look at some pretty good examples:

1. **Butterfly Garden**: A butterfly garden is designed to attract beautiful butterflies. You can plant colorful flowers that butterflies love, like daisies and milkweed. By creating a butterfly garden, you can watch them flutter around and land on the flowers, looking for food.
2. **Fairy Garden:** A fairy garden is a magical garden full of tiny decorations and plants. You will be creating a mini-world for fairies to visit by using small houses, tiny furniture, and even tiny fairy figurines. Planting small flowers, like forget-me-nots and pansies, adds to the enchantment. Who knows? You might find a fairy hiding in your garden one day.
3. **Pizza Garden:** A pizza garden has to be the best idea ever thought of. Here, you can grow ingredients to make as many pizzas as you want. You can plant tomato plants for the sauce, basil for the herbs, bell peppers for toppings, and even onions. It's a garden full of the delicious things you need to make your very own homemade pizzas.

Chapter 4: Herbs and Flowers

Herbs are the cool cousins of the plant world. They are small but mighty, with leaves you can use to make your food taste delicious. Pizza with oregano sprinkled on top is a great example. Most herbs also have powers you probably didn't know about. Some herbs, like chamomile, can help you relax and have a good night's sleep. Others, like peppermint, can make your tummy feel better when it is upset. Flowers, on the other hand, are nature's artists. They paint the world with their breathtaking beauty. From the happy faces of daisies to the delicate petals of roses, flowers come in all shapes, sizes, and colors. They're a living example of nature's artistry.

The Value of Growing Herbs and Flowers in Your Garden

1. **Colors and Beauty**: When you grow herbs and flowers, you get to have all sorts of colors in your garden. It could be filled with bright red, jolly yellow, and pretty purple flowers.
2. **Fragrances and Scents:** Have you ever smelled a flower and automatically felt better? Flowers have different scents; some are fresh or even spicy. Some flowers smell deliciously sweet, while others are more calming. Growing flowers in your garden means you get to enjoy all of these scents and make your garden smell fantastic for anyone who decides to visit.

3. **Helping Bees and Butterflies:** Bees and butterflies are more important to the world than you think, and they need all the help they can get for their super-important mission. They help plants by moving pollen from one flower to another, and this helps new plants grow and make more food. By growing herbs and flowers in your garden, you'll feed these pollinators with as much nectar as needed. They'll come buzzing and flying around, making your garden their favorite hangout spot.
4. **Tasty Flavors**: Herbs are also flavor boosters for your food. Have you ever tried fresh basil in your pasta sauce or sprinkling mint leaves in your lemonade? Growing herbs in your garden means you can add all of these flavors and more to your meals. You'll have a mini herb store right outside.
5. **Sharing and Gifting**: You get to pick a bunch of beautiful flowers from your garden and give them to someone special. You can make someone's day brighter with a very simple gift.

Useful Herbs and Flowers to Grow in Your Garden

Whether you have a green thumb or are just starting your first garden, these herbs and flowers have been specifically designed for children's gardens. Here, you have different herbs and flowers that are easy to care for, very pretty to look at, and lovely to smell. Take a look:

Herbs for Children's Gardens

Basil.[57]

Basil (Ocimum basilicum)

- **Description**: Basil is a unique herb with leaves that smell and taste amazing. It comes in different types, like sweet basil, lemon basil, and purple basil.

- **Planting:** Plant basil in soil that gets lots of sunlight. Make sure the soil is not too wet, and there is some space between each plant.
- **Watering**: Give basil enough water to keep the soil moist but not soggy. Don't forget to water it regularly, especially on hot days.
- **Tip:** If you want more basil leaves for cooking, pinch off the little flowers that grow on top.

Mint (Mentha spp.)

- **Description**: Mint is a refreshing herb that smells just like a cool breeze. There are different kinds, but the most popular are peppermint and spearmint.
- **Planting**: Plant mint in a pot or a separate part of the garden because it spreads quickly. It likes some shade, as it doesn't like getting too hot.
- **Watering:** Keep the soil damp but not soaked. Mint likes to drink water regularly, especially in hot weather.
- **Tip:** To make sure the mint stays bushy and doesn't get too tall, trim the stems regularly.

Chives (Allium schoenoprasum)

- **Description**: Chives look like spring onions, but they are tinier with pretty purple flowers. They taste delicious, too.
- **Planting:** Put chives in areas with some sunlight, but not too much. Leave space between each plant.
- **Watering:** Chives need regular drinks of water, but let the soil dry out a bit between watering.
- **Tip:** Snip the long leaves from the bottom to help new leaves grow. It's also a good idea to remove the flowers before they bloom.

Dill (Anethum graveolens)

- **Description:** Dill has feathery leaves and bright yellow flowers that butterflies love.
- **Planting:** Plant dill in a place that gets lots of sun. Leave some space between each plant.

- **Watering:** Give dill enough water so the soil stays moist but not too wet.
- **Tip:** Harvest the leaves and seeds often to keep the plant healthy and prevent it from flowering too quickly.

Lemon Balm (Melissa officinalis)
- **Description:** Lemon balm has cute little white flowers and leaves that smell like lemons.
- **Planting:** Put lemon balm in a slightly sunny spot. Leave a bit of space between each plant.
- **Watering:** Keep the soil moist by watering regularly.
- **Tip:** Trim the plant often, especially the top, to make it grow fuller and not too tall.

Flowers for Children's Gardens
Marigold (Tagetes spp.)

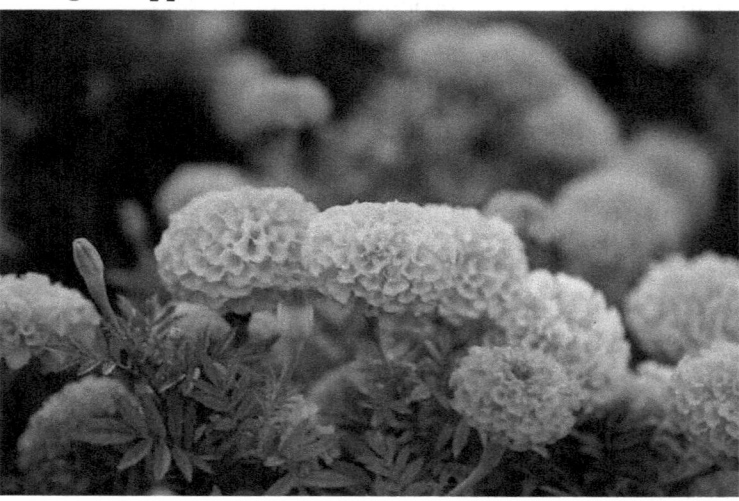

Marigolds.[58]

- **Description:** Marigolds have flowers in bright colors like yellow, orange, and red. They look just like tiny suns.
- **Planting:** Place marigolds in an area that gets lots of sun. Give each plant enough space to grow.
- **Watering:** Water marigolds when the soil feels dry, and don't forget to give them a drink regularly.

- **Tip**: If you remove the flowers that have finished blooming, you'll make room for new ones to grow.

Sunflower (Helianthus annuus)

- **Description**: Sunflowers are tall plants with big, happy flowers that follow the sun as it moves across the sky.
- **Planting**: Plant sunflower seeds directly in soil that gets lots of sun. Give each plant some space to grow because they can get massive.
- **Watering**: Water sunflowers when the soil feels dry. They like a good drink regularly.
- **Tip**: Use sticks or supports to help the tall sunflowers stand up straight.

Nasturtium (Tropaeolum spp.)

- **Description**: Nasturtiums have flowers in beautiful colors like red, orange, and yellow. They also taste a little spicy.
- **Planting**: Plant nasturtiums under a bit of sun, but not too much. Give each plant some space to spread out.
- **Watering**: Water nasturtiums when the soil feels dry. They like to stay a bit dry between watering.
- **Tip**: If you remove the flowers that have gone over, more new flowers will keep growing.

Zinnia (Zinnia spp.)

- **Description**: Zinnias come in many colors, like pink, purple, red, and orange.
- **Planting**: Plant zinnias where they'll get lots of sun. Each plant needs its own space to grow properly.
- **Watering**: Water zinnias when the soil feels dry. They like regular drinks of water.
- **Tip**: If you remove the flowers that have finished blooming, new ones will keep popping up.

Pansy (Viola spp.)

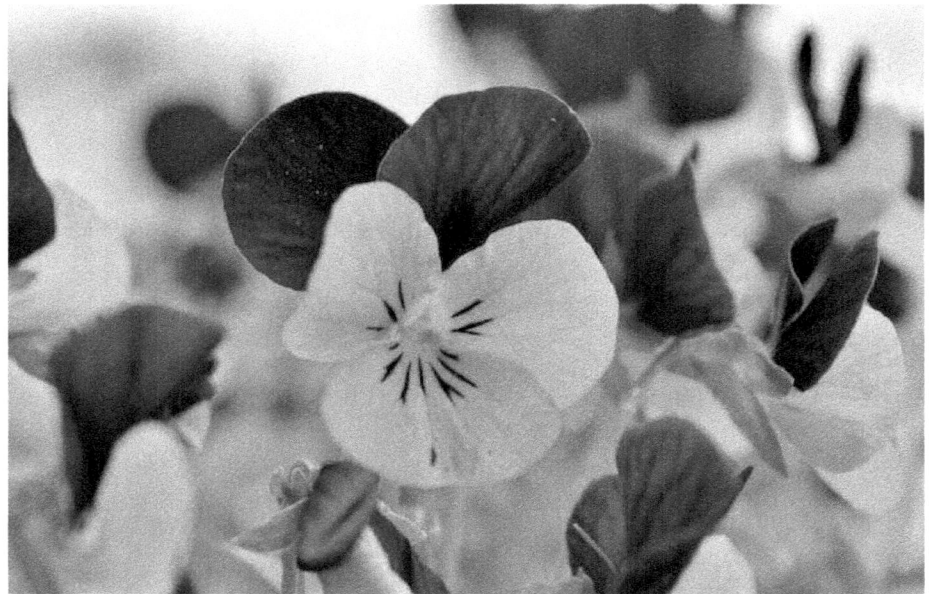

Pansy.[59]

- **Description:** Pansies have flowers with pretty faces in colors like purple, yellow, blue, and white. They look like they're smiling at you.
- **Planting:** Pansies like sunny spots and a bit of shade sometimes. They also need space to grow.
- **Watering:** Water pansies when the soil feels dry. They like to stay a little dry between watering.
- **Tip:** Pinch off the tall parts of the plant to help it grow bushier. And if you remove the flowers that are done, more flowers will keep blooming.

Using Herbs in the Kitchen

Herbs add flavor and aroma to dishes, take you on a ride through the culinary world, and let you get creative in the kitchen. Here are some herbs and recipes you can experiment with:

- **Basil:** Basil has a sweet and slightly peppery flavor. It's perfect for adding to salads, pasta dishes, and sandwiches. You can try making caprese skewers by threading cherry tomatoes, small mozzarella balls, and fresh basil leaves onto skewers. Drizzle with a little olive oil and balsamic glaze for a tasty and colorful snack.

- **Mint:** Mint has a refreshing and cool taste. You can add it to your drinks, salads, and desserts. A fun idea is to make minty lemonade by squeezing fresh lemon juice, adding some chopped mint leaves, and sweetening it with a bit of honey or sugar. Mix it all together with water and ice, and it's ready to go.
- **Chives:** Chives have a mild onion flavor. They can be sprinkled on soups, baked potatoes, and scrambled eggs. You can make cheesy chive omelets by whisking eggs, adding chopped chives, grated cheese, and a pinch of salt. Cook the mixture in a pan until it sets, and enjoy a delicious and protein-packed breakfast.
- **Dill:** Dill has a unique flavor that is often linked to pickles. It pairs well with fish, potatoes, and salads. Try preparing a creamy dill dip by mixing Greek yogurt, chopped dill, garlic powder, and a squeeze of lemon juice. Serve it with carrot sticks, cucumber slices, or whole-grain crackers for something healthy and tasty.
- **Rosemary:** Rosemary has a strong and aromatic flavor. It's great for seasoning roasted vegetables, chicken, and potatoes. You can try rosemary roasted potatoes by tossing diced potatoes with olive oil, minced rosemary leaves, salt, and pepper. Bake in the oven until crispy and golden brown.

Design Ideas for Your Herb and Flower Garden

1. Rainbow Meadow

Create a rainbow in your garden by planting flowers of different colors in rows or clusters. Start with red flowers like roses or tulips, then move on to orange marigolds, yellow sunflowers, green ferns, blue pansies, indigo petunias, and finally, purple lavender.

2. Colorful Containers

If you are using pots or containers, paint them in bright, fun colors and shades of red, yellow, or even blue. Then, plant different flowers in each container, matching the colors of the pots. For example, you could plant red geraniums in the red pot, yellow marigolds in the yellow pot, and blue lobelia in the blue pot.

3. **Pollinator Paradise**

   Design a garden that attracts pollinators like bees and butterflies. Choose flowers that are both colorful and rich in nectar, such as bee balm, coneflowers, and sunflowers. You can also add some herbs like lavender, mint, or basil, which pollinators love, too.

4. **Sensory Sensation**

   Try building a garden that engages all your senses. Choose flowers with different textures; some common ones are woolly lamb's ear or velvety pansies. Then include plants with interesting smells, maybe scented geraniums or chocolate-scented cosmos. You can even add wind chimes or a small water feature for soothing sounds.

Chapter 5: Harvest Time

It's time to celebrate all the hard work you've put into your garden and get ready to harvest your hard-earned rewards. Harvesting means picking the fruit, vegetables, and herbs grown in your garden. It's an exciting and rewarding moment in gardening. You've watered, nurtured, and watched your plants grow, and now it's time to enjoy the fruits of your labor. It's a special moment when you see your hard work transform into something you can taste, smell, and enjoy.

Harvesting allows you to see the hard work you've put into your garden.[60]

Knowing When to Harvest

It's easy to tell when fruit, vegetables, and herbs are ready to be harvested if you know what to look for. Here are some clues:

- **Color:** Fruit and vegetables that are ripe have obvious, bright colors. For example, strawberries turn bright red when they're ready to be picked, and carrots become a rich orange color. So, keep an eye out for colors that pop.
- **Size Matters:** As fruit and vegetables grow, they get bigger and reach a certain size when they're just right. For instance, zucchinis should be about 6-8 inches long before being picked. So, compare the size of your plants to pictures or samples to see if they're ready.
- **Ripeness:** Ripeness is all about taste and texture. Some fruits and vegetables become sweeter and juicier as they ripen. For example, when watermelons are ready, they sound hollow when you tap them and have a sweet aroma. Tomatoes are ripe when firm but slightly soft when gently squeezed. And herbs are at their best when they have a strong scent. Trust your senses to tell you if something is ripe and ready to go into your basket.

Of course, not everything in the garden ripens at the same time. Some plants take longer, while others are ready sooner. So, check your plants regularly to catch them at their tastiest moments.

How to Harvest Different Fruits, Vegetables, and Herbs

- **Cutting Crops**

When it's time to harvest different crops from the garden, you can use a few methods. You use scissors or garden snips to carefully cut crops like lettuce. Hold the stem of the lettuce gently and snip it close to the base. Remember to cut only what you need so the plant can keep growing and producing more.

- **Picking Fruits and Vegetable**

For fruit and vegetables like tomatoes, strawberries, or cucumbers, you use your hands to pick them. Hold the fruit or vegetable gently and give it a little twist or tug. If it comes off the plant easily, it's ready to be harvested.

- **Gently Pulling**

Some crops, like carrots or radishes, are pulled straight from the ground. Hold the green leaves firmly near the base and give them a gentle pull. The root vegetables will come out with a satisfying "pop." Just be careful not to pull too hard, or the leaves might come off without the root.

To pick strawberries, just hold them gently and give them a tug.[61]

- **Snipping Herbs**

Herbs like basil, mint, or parsley have their own special techniques. The best time to harvest herbs is in the morning after the dew has dried but before it gets too hot. This is when the herbs have the most flavor. To harvest, use scissors or garden snips to snip off the leaves or stems just above a set of leaves. This way, the plant can grow and produce more leaves.

If you have more herbs than you can use right away, you can preserve them for later. One way is by drying them. Gather a bunch of herb stems, tie them together with string, and hang them upside down in a cool, dry place. Once dry and crisp, crumble the leaves into a jar for future use. Another option is freezing herbs. Chop them up, place them in ice cube trays, and fill each cube with water. Pop them in the freezer, and when you need herbs for a recipe, grab a herb cube and toss it in.

Taking Care of Your Harvest

Caring for your harvest keeps it fresh and delicious. When you harvest anything, you want to avoid bruising or damaging your precious goodies to keep them fresh for longer. Fruits and vegetables can get bruised or squished if you're not careful, making them go bad faster. But when you treat them gently, they stay nice and tasty.

Besides, you've put so much effort into growing your garden, and you want to enjoy the fruits (and vegetables) of your labor. By handling them carefully, you show respect for all your hard work. Plus, eating something that looks as good as it tastes is more fun. Bring a basket or a container when you go out to harvest. You can gently place your fruit, vegetables, and herbs inside, keeping them safe and snug. Baskets or containers protect your produce and prevent them from getting squished or bumped as you move around the garden.

Harvest Recipes

You can create delicious meals using the ingredients you've grown. Here are some simple and easy recipes that you can try at home:

- **Garden Veggie Pizza**

For this recipe, you'll need a pizza crust, tomato sauce, and as many fresh vegetables as you can get from your garden. Start by spreading the tomato sauce on the crust. Then, get creative and add your favorite garden produce, like tomatoes, bell peppers, onions, and even some basil leaves. Top it off with a sprinkle of cheese, and ask a grown-up to help you bake it until the cheese is nice and bubbly.

- **Fresh Strawberry Parfait**

This is the easiest recipe for your garden-grown strawberries. Grab a clear glass or a fancy cup and layer it with fresh strawberries, a dollop of yogurt, and a sprinkle of granola or crushed cookies. Repeat the layers until your cup is full, and you're good to go.

- **Garden Veggie Wraps**

For these tasty wraps, you'll need large lettuce leaves (like romaine or butter lettuce) from your garden, sliced cucumbers, shredded carrots, and any other veggies you love. Spread some creamy hummus or cream cheese on the lettuce leaf, then pile on the veggies. Roll it up like a burrito, and you've got a garden-fresh wrap ready to eat.

- **Cheesy Zucchini Bites**

Zucchinis are a fantastic garden vegetable to use in this recipe. Grate a zucchini and squeeze out any excess moisture. Mix it with breadcrumbs, grated cheese, an egg (with the help of a grown-up), and some seasonings like salt and pepper. Shape the mixture into little patties and cook them in a pan until golden brown on both sides.

- **Stuffed Bell Peppers**

Bell peppers are colorful and make a great container for stuffing. Cut the tops off the peppers and remove the seeds. Mix cooked rice, diced tomatoes, corn kernels, cooked ground meat (like beef or turkey), and some shredded cheese in a bowl. Spoon the mixture into the hollowed-out bell peppers. Place them on a baking sheet and get a grown-up to bake them in the oven until the peppers are tender and the filling is hot and bubbly.

Cooking is a way to express your creativity, so feel free to switch up these recipes to suit your taste and the ingredients you have on hand. Experimenting with the flavors in your garden is a wonderful way to appreciate the magic of growing your own food, so have fun in the kitchen and enjoy the rewards of your garden harvest.

Chapter 6: Garden Friends and Pests

This chapter is for the tiny creatures that play a role of some kind in all the green spaces. You'll learn about the helpful and not-so-friendly ones and how they can affect your garden. Every farm or garden has a whole community of insects and animals buzzing around or scurrying about. Some of them are your garden champions, like bees and ladybugs, who work hard to pollinate flowers and eat harmful pests that can damage your plants. The others are critters that cause trouble. These are the pests, like aphids or slugs, that munch on your plants and make them sick. They're not the best guests at your garden party – but don't worry, you can manage them.

By learning about the different types of insects and animals in your garden, you can become an expert detective who knows how to identify them, understand their behaviors, and determine whether they're beneficial or harmful. That way, you can create a garden where the good bugs are welcome and the pests are bounced at the door.

Beneficial Insects

Here are some beneficial insects and pollinators you can find in gardens, along with tips on how to attract them:

- **Bees**

Bees are fantastic pollinators.[63]

Pollinators are like the superheroes of the plant world! Bees are a famous example, but butterflies, hummingbirds, and even some bats are pollinators!

Here's what they do: when they go from flower to flower to drink nectar, which is a sweet liquid that flowers make, they get pollen on their bodies. Pollen is a yellow, powdery substance that plants need to make seeds.

When a pollinator visits another flower, the pollen rubs off onto that flower. This helps the flower create seeds that can grow into new plants. It's like the pollinators are helping the flowers send messages to each other so they can make more flowers! Thanks to pollinators, we have lots of fruits and vegetables to eat, and so do many animals in the wild. So, next time you see a bee buzzing around flowers, remember it's doing a super important job!

So, be sure to plant various flowering plants with different shapes and colors to attract bees to your garden. Bees love flowers like sunflowers, lavender, and wildflowers. Also, keep a shallow water source nearby, like a small dish with stones for them to land on, so they can stay hydrated while they fly around doing their thing.

- **Ladybugs**

Ladybugs eat harmful pests.[68]

Ladybugs are adorable and helpful insects that eat harmful pests like aphids. To attract ladybugs, grow plants like dill, fennel, and marigold. You can also create a ladybug house by tying together a few small sticks or bamboo pieces and placing them in a sheltered spot. Ladybugs will move in as soon as they find it and help keep your garden pest-free.

- **Butterflies**

Butterflies are not only beautiful but also important pollinators. Plant nectar-rich flowers such as milkweed, zinnias, and lantanas to attract butterflies. Create a butterfly puddling station by filling a shallow dish with sand and keeping it moist. Butterflies love to sip water and extract minerals from the damp sand.

- **Ground Beetles**

Ground beetles are nighttime hunters that feast on slugs, snails, and other pests. To attract ground beetles, prepare a tiny house for them with mulch or leaf piles. They also like plants with small flowers, such as daisies and asters. By keeping your garden diverse and setting up hiding spots, you'll let these beetles know they are welcome to stay and help.

Ground beetles feast on pests.[64]

- **Lacewings**

Lacewings are delicate insects that consume aphids, mealybugs, and other soft-bodied pests. Plant pollen and nectar-rich flowers such as dandelions, cosmos, and coreopsis to attract lacewings. Or you can buy lacewing eggs or larvae from garden supply stores and release them to grow and multiply in your garden.

- **Hoverflies**

Hoverflies, also known as flower flies, are excellent pollinators and aphid-eaters. To attract hoverflies, include plants like yarrow, daisies, and calendula in your garden. They love flowers with flat tops where they can land easily. Avoid using chemical pesticides because hoverflies are sensitive to them and may get sick.

Harmful Pests

Here are some common garden pests and tips on how to manage them:

- **Aphids**

Aphids are small, sap-sucking insects that can damage your plants. To deal with aphids, encourage natural predators like ladybugs and lacewings by planting flowers that attract them, such as daisies and fennel. You can also spray a mixture of water and mild dish soap onto affected plants to chase away aphids.

- **Whiteflies**

Whiteflies feed on plant sap.[65]

Whiteflies are tiny, flying insects that feed on plant sap and can cause leaf yellowing and wilting. To control whiteflies, bring in natural enemies like parasitic wasps and predatory beetles into your garden. Yellow sticky traps placed near infested plants can also help catch adult whiteflies.

- **Slugs and Snails**

Slugs and snails are nighttime pests that can chew holes in leaves and stems. To control them, physical barriers like copper tape or *diatomaceous earth* should be put up around vulnerable plants. Diatomaceous earth is a super cool, powdery substance that comes from the fossilized remains of tiny, aquatic creatures called diatoms. Think of diatoms as really small algae that have a hard shell. Over millions of years, these shells piled up on the bottom of oceans or lakes and turned into a kind of rock. When this rock is ground up, it turns into a fine, white powder –that's diatomaceous earth!

It's sort of like magic dust for gardeners because it helps keep bugs away from plants without using chemicals. It works by sticking to the bugs that crawl over it, and since it's sharp on a microscopic level, it scratches the bugs and makes them lose water and dry out. But don't worry, it's safe for people and pets when used properly!

You can also set up slug traps filled with beer or yeast solution to attract and drown them. Handpicking them off plants in the evening or early morning and disposing of them can also be effective.

How to Identify and Manage Pests

These are a few methods you can try to help you identify and manage pests in your garden.

Physical Control

1. Look closely at your plants and check for any signs of pests, like holes in leaves or chewed stems.
2. If you spot pests, you can physically remove them by gently picking them off with your hands or using tweezers.
3. For larger pests like slugs or snails, you can set up barriers around the plants using materials like crushed eggshells or diatomaceous earth. These two things create a rough surface that the pests don't like to crawl over.
4. You can also set up traps, like shallow dishes filled with beer or yeast solution, to attract and catch pests like slugs. Remember to check the traps regularly and toss any trapped pests you find.

Safety Guidelines

- Always wash your hands thoroughly after handling pests.
- If you're not really sure how to handle a particular pest, ask an adult for help.

Biological Control

1. Learn about the good insects that can help control pests in your garden, such as ladybugs or praying mantises.
2. Create a welcoming environment for these insects by planting flowers that attract them, like daisies or marigolds.
3. You can also buy or build special houses or shelters designed for them.
4. Once the beneficial insects move in, they naturally eat the pests and help keep their numbers in check.

Safety Guidelines
- Be gentle and careful when handling beneficial insects to avoid harming them.
- Avoid chemical pesticides, as they can harm beneficial insects and your garden ecosystem.

Cultural Control
1. Practice good garden hygiene by regularly removing fallen leaves, weeds, and dirt. Pests often hide in these areas.
2. Rotate your crops each year. This means planting different types of plants in different spots. It prevents pests from building up in the soil and attacking the same plants year after year.
3. Water your plants properly. Some pests like to hang out on wet leaves, so it's better to water your plants at the base and avoid overwatering.

Safety Guidelines
- Use gloves to protect your hands from sharp objects or thorns when cleaning up garden debris.

Non-Chemical, Holistic Control Methods

1. Make your own natural pest repellents. For example, you can mix water and mild liquid soap to create a spray that scares off pests like aphids.
2. Plant companion plants that repel pests. Some plants, like marigolds or basil, have natural properties that pests don't like.
3. Create a healthy garden ecosystem by attracting birds, butterflies, and other beneficial wildlife. They can help control pests naturally.

Safety Guidelines
- Follow the instructions and measurements carefully when making homemade pest repellents.
- Ask an adult for help when handling or mixing ingredients.
- Observe and check on your garden regularly because pest problems can arise at any time.

Chapter 7: Tips and Troubleshooting

By now, you probably agree that gardening is a neat way to get your own plants, whether beautiful flowers or juicy vegetables. But this method is not foolproof; sometimes, plants have problems, too. Don't worry, though, because most of these problems can be fixed with some know-how and simple actions. In this chapter, you will look at some common issues that gardeners usually face, how to recognize these problems, and what to do about them. This should get you started:

Pests

- **Recognize:** Look for tiny insects or holes in the leaves.
- **Action:** Pick off pests by hand or use natural sprays like soapy water.

Weeds

- **Recognize:** Notice unwanted plants growing among your flowers or vegetables.
- **Action**: Pull out weeds by hand, *making sure to get the roots.*

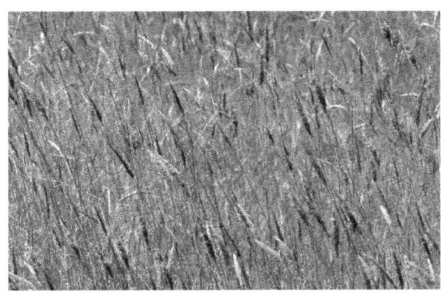

Weeds can harm your plants.[66]

Diseases

- **Recognize:** Observe spots, discoloration, or wilting on plants.
- **Action:** Remove infected leaves or plants, and use organic fungicides if it looks too bad.

Overwatering

- **Recognize:** Watch for waterlogged soil or yellowing, droopy leaves.
- **Action:** Reduce watering and let the soil dry out between watering.

Underwatering

- **Recognize:** Look for dry, crispy leaves or wilted plants.
- **Action:** Water plants thoroughly and regularly, making sure the soil is moist.

Nutrient Deficiency

- **Recognize**: Notice yellowing or stunted growth in plants.
- **Action:** Add organic fertilizers or compost to top up the nutrients in the soil.

Sunburn

- **Recognize:** See brown, dry patches on leaves or stems.
- **Action:** Set up shade for the plant during the hottest parts of the day.

Poor Soil

- **Recognize**: The soil is dry, hard, or dull.
- **Action**: Add compost or organic matter to improve soil quality.

Poor Pollination

- **Recognize:** Observe small or weirdly shaped fruits or flowers falling off.
- **Action:** Attract pollinators like bees by planting flowers or using bee-friendly sprays.

Improper Pruning

- **Recognize**: Notice uneven or damaged branches on plants.
- **Action**: Use clean pruning shears to properly trim plants. Be sure to know where to cut each plant. If you are unsure, ask an adult for help.

Seasonal Challenges

Each season brings its own unique obstacles, from unpredictable weather to nasty pests. Still, as always, there's nothing to worry about because, with some knowledge and clever tricks, you can breeze through these challenges and have a successful garden all year round.

Spring

- **Challenge**: Unpredictable weather and temperature changes.
- **What to Do:** Start planting seeds indoors or in a greenhouse before taking them outside. Protect young plants from cold snaps by covering them with a special cloth or plastic cover. Move potted plants indoors if you are expecting frost.

Summer

- **Challenge**: Hot temperatures and a lack of water.
- **What to Do:** Water your plants deeply and regularly; it is best to water in the early morning or evening when it's cooler. Put a layer of mulch (like straw or wood chips) around your plants to help keep the soil moist. Make shade for your plants using umbrellas or a temporary shade cloth.

Fall

- **Challenge**: Shorter days and cooler weather.
- **What to Do:** Plant cool-season crops like lettuce, spinach, and kale that like the cooler temperatures. Harvest ripe fruits and

vegetables before the first frost. Use covers or plastic tunnels to protect plants from frost and keep them growing longer.

Winter

- **Challenge:** Freezing temperatures and frost.
- **What to Do:** Bring potted plants indoors or into a greenhouse to keep them warm. Put a layer of mulch around the base of plants to protect their roots. Consider planting cold-hardy vegetables like carrots that can survive the cold.

All Seasons

- **Challenge**: Weeds and pests.
- **What to Do**: Pull out weeds regularly by grabbing them at the root. Attract helpful insects like ladybugs and praying mantises by planting flowers they like. Use natural pest control methods like planting certain plants together or using friendly bugs to eat the bad bugs.

Preventive Measures in Gardening

Being a gardener is more than putting seeds in the ground and watching them grow. A gardener also cares for their plants and ensures they are healthy and happy. Just like you visit the doctor for check-ups, your plants need regular health checks, too. By performing routine garden health checks, you can look for signs of trouble or damage to your plants and take action to keep them alive. Here are some inspection routines you should practice as a good gardener:

Daily Visual Inspection

- Look closely at your plants every day.
- Check for any wilting or drooping leaves, which could mean the plant needs water.
- Look for any holes or bite marks on the leaves, which may indicate pests.

Leaf Color Check

- Examine the color of the leaves.
- Healthy leaves should be green and vibrant.
- If you see yellowing, browning, or spots on the leaves, it could be a sign of a problem.

Stem and Branch Check
- Check the stems and branches of your plants.
- Look for any cracks, breaks, or signs of damage.
- Make sure the stems and branches are strong and do not bend or droop too much.

Flower and Fruit Inspection
- Look at the flowers and fruits on your plants.
- Check if they are developing properly and not wilting or falling off prematurely.
- Look for any signs of discoloration, spots, or mold on the flowers or fruits.

Soil Moisture Test
- Gently touch the soil around your plants with your finger.
- Check if it feels dry or too wet. Plants need moist soil, not soggy or bone-dry soil.

Pest Patrol
- Keep an eye out for any bugs or insects on your plants.
- Look for small crawling creatures or flying insects around the leaves or soil.
- If you spot any pests, take note and ask an adult for help identifying and dealing with them.

Weed Control
- Scan your garden for any unwanted plants (weeds) growing among your plants.
- Pull out any weeds you find by gently tugging them from the base.
- Make sure to remove the entire weed, including the roots.

Effective Gardening Tips

Regular Gardening Maintenance
- **Tip:** Take care of your garden regularly to keep it healthy.
- **What to Do:** Remove weeds, dead leaves, and debris from your garden beds. Prune plants to remove dead or damaged branches. Keep an eye out for pests, and take action as soon as possible if

you see any.

Record Keeping

- **Tip:** Keep a record of your garden activities and observations.
- **What to Do:** Use a notebook or a gardening journal to write down important information like planting dates, plant varieties, and any changes you notice in your plants. This will help you track progress and learn from your experiences.

Soil Testing

Checking your soil's health can help you ensure your plants get the right nutrients.[67]

- **Tip:** Check your soil's health to ensure your plants have the right nutrients.
- **What to Do:** Use a soil testing kit or take a sample to a lab for testing. It will help you understand if your soil needs any amendments, like adding compost or fertilizer, to make it better for your plants.

Watering Techniques

- **Tip:** Water your plants properly to give them the right amount of moisture.
- **What to Do**: Use a watering can or a hose with a gentle spray nozzle. Water the base of the plants, avoiding the leaves. Water deeply but less frequently, allowing the soil to dry out slightly between waterings. This encourages plants to develop strong roots.

Composting
- **Tip:** Turn your kitchen scraps into nutrient-rich compost for your garden.
- **What to Do:** Collect fruit and vegetable scraps, coffee grounds, and eggshells. Put them in a compost bin or pile. Add some leaves, grass clippings, or shredded paper. Turn the pile occasionally. Over time, it will break down into compost that you can use to feed your soil.

Planting for Pollinators
- **Tip:** Help bees and butterflies by planting flowers they love.
- **What to Do:** Choose colorful flowers like zinnias, cosmos, and coneflowers that attract pollinators. Plant them in your garden or in pots on your balcony or windowsill. In no time, you'll be getting a lot of beautiful, helpful visitors.

Organic Gardening Methods

Organic gardening is a way of growing plants and food without using any synthetic (fake) chemicals like pesticides and fertilizers. Instead, it focuses on using natural methods to care for plants and create a healthy ecosystem in the garden. This is good because it protects the environment, keeps you healthy, and supports the balance of nature. Here are some quick and easy organic gardening methods to get you on your way to becoming an eco-friendly gardener:

Companion Planting
- **Tip:** Some plants make great friends with each other and help each other grow.
- **What to Do:** Plant certain flowers, herbs, or vegetables together to protect each other from pests or provide mutual benefits. For example, plant marigolds near tomatoes to keep pests away or grow basil near tomatoes to increase root growth, plant size, and production. Planting thyme near strawberries can increase the chances of a good harvest. Thyme is an herb that attracts bees.

  Remember: Bees are important for pollinating strawberry flowers. Sunflowers and pumpkins are another good combination. Sunflowers are tall and can provide shade for pumpkin plants, which helps keep the soil cool and moist. These are just a few examples, but many other companion plants can be grown together. Try to experiment and observe how different plants can help each other, and you might just discover something you could teach other gardeners.

Use Neem Oil

- **Tip:** Neem oil is a natural way to keep bugs away from your plants.
- **What to Do**: To make neem oil spray for plants, you'll need neem oil, mild liquid soap (like dish soap), and water. Mix 1 teaspoon of neem oil and 1/2 teaspoon of mild liquid soap in a small container. The soap helps the oil mix with water. Get a spray bottle and fill it with 4 cups of water. Pour the neem oil and soap mixture into the spray bottle. Close the spray bottle tightly and shake it well to mix everything together. Spray this mixture on the leaves, stems, and other plant parts with bugs. Make sure to spray all over the plants, including the tops and bottoms of the leaves. This spray will help eliminate bugs like aphids, mites, whiteflies, and caterpillars. Use the spray every 7-14 days or when you see bugs coming back.

Chapter 8: Fun Garden Projects

Gardening can be a hands-on adventure that lets you actively engage with the garden and have a blast, but only if you are open to the possibilities. So many fun garden projects will spark your creativity, teach you new things, and bring a new kind of life to your outdoor space. See these projects as quests where you get to create, explore, and learn from nature. There's so much more to gardening than you expect! From creating garden art to building a bug hotel, each project will offer a unique opportunity to get your hands dirty, tap into your imagination, and work closely with the natural world.

Creating Garden Art

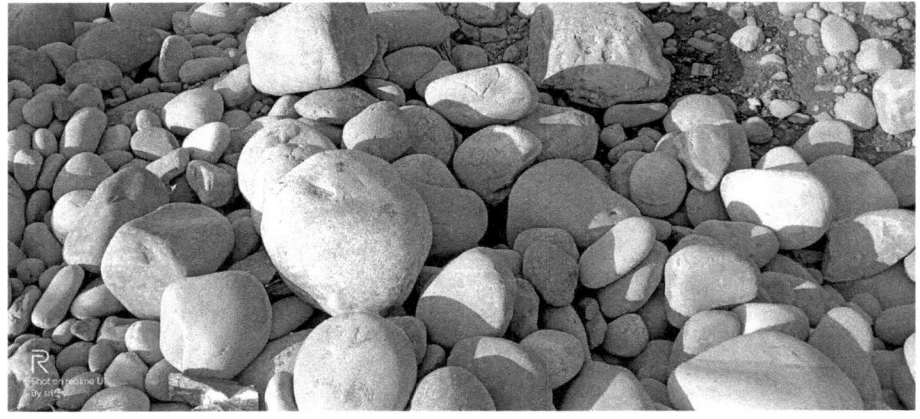

Use pebbles to create garden art.[68]

Materials Needed:
- Smooth rocks or pebbles
- Acrylic paint
- Paintbrushes
- Sealant (optional)
- Clear varnish or outdoor Mod Podge (optional)

Instructions:
1. **Collect Rocks**: Go on a hunt for smooth rocks or pebbles of different sizes and shapes. Make sure they are clean and dry before starting.
2. **Design Ideas:** Think about what kind of garden art you want to create. It could be ladybugs, flowers, or even colorful patterns.
3. **Paint Your Rocks:** Lay out a protective surface, like a newspaper or a tablecloth. Using acrylic paint to bring your design ideas to life, apply a base coat on the rock, and then add details and colors to create your desired design. Don't forget to let each layer of paint dry before adding more.
4. **Decorate Your Garden**: Once your painted rocks are completely dry, it's time to display them in your garden. Find the best spot where you want to add some garden art. You can place them in a flower bed, a garden path, or a potted plant. Arrange the rocks in a way that makes the beauty of your garden pop and brings a touch of creativity to the space.
5. **Seal the Artwork (Adult Supervision Required)**: Apply a sealant to protect your garden art from the weather. Ask an adult to help you with this step. Use a clear varnish or outdoor Mod Podge to seal the painted rocks. Apply a thin, even layer, and let it dry completely.
6. **Enjoy and Learn**: Observe how your garden art enhances the total beauty of your garden. Take note of any changes or reactions from insects or birds that visit your garden art. Learn about different insects or animals that may be attracted to your art and their role in the ecosystem.

Setting Up a Theme Garden

Designing a theme garden is a fun way to create a garden space with plants that have a specific message or story. It's very easy, and anyone can do it. To get started:

1. **Choose a Theme:** The first step is to pick a theme for your garden. It could be anything you like, from butterflies, dinosaurs, and fairies to even your favorite book or movie. Just think about what you love and what makes you excited.

2. **Research Your Theme:** Once you have a theme in mind, do some research to learn more about it. Look for books and websites, or ask an adult for help. Find out what kinds of plants, colors, and decorations are associated with your theme.

3. **Plan Your Garden:** Draw a simple garden layout on a piece of paper. Think about where you want to put different plants and decorations. Remember to leave enough space for your plants to grow.

4. **Choose Plants:** Now, it's time to pick the plants that go with your theme. For example, if you have chosen a butterfly theme, you could plant flowers that attract butterflies, like lavender or coneflowers. If you have chosen a dinosaur theme, you could go with leafy plants that give off a prehistoric jungle vibe. Kale, lettuce, and basil are good examples.

5. **Add Some Decorations:** Decorations can make your theme garden even more realistic. You can make your own decorations using craft materials or find ready-made ones at a store. For example, if you choose a fairy theme, you could add some small fairy statues or a mini fairy house.

6. **Plant and Care for Your Garden:** Now it's time to start planting. Follow the instructions on the plant tags or ask an adult for help. Make sure to water your plants regularly and give them enough sunlight. Weeds can compete with your plants for water and nutrients, so you must keep an eye out for them and remove them when you see them.

Garden Projects

The garden projects you'll find here are not only fun, but they also teach you important concepts. Here are some projects that will add a bit of knowledge to your gardening experience:

Water Cycle Project

The water cycle explains how water moves around the Earth. You can learn about it by creating your own mini-water cycle in a jar. Here's how:

1. Find a clear glass jar and fill it about one-third full with water.
2. Place a small plate or plastic wrap on top of the jar, making sure it's tightly sealed.
3. Put the jar in a sunny spot, like a windowsill, and watch what happens over a few days.
4. As the sun heats the water, the water evaporates, and you'll see water droplets forming on the bottom of the plate or plastic wrap. The droplets are the result of a process called condensation and symbolize the clouds.
5. After a while, the droplets will fall and return to the water in the jar, symbolizing rain falling from the clouds. This part of the cycle is called *precipitation.*

This project shows how water evaporates from the earth's surface, forms clouds, and then returns as rain, completing the water cycle.

Butterfly Life Cycle Project

Butterflies go through a fascinating transformation called metamorphosis. You can learn about their life cycle by creating a butterfly garden and observing their stages. Here's what you can do:

1. Find a sunny spot in your garden or a large pot and fill it with soil.
2. Plant some butterfly-friendly flowers like milkweed, which is food for caterpillars, and other nectar-rich flowers like zinnias or marigolds.
3. Look for butterfly eggs or caterpillars on the milkweed leaves. If you find any, gently place them in a jar with some leaves.
4. Watch the caterpillars as they eat and grow. They will molt (shed their skin) several times and get bigger.
5. Once they stop eating and get bigger, they will form a chrysalis, a protective covering made of silk.

6. Keep watching the chrysalis; after some time, you'll notice a beautiful butterfly come out of it.
7. Release the butterfly in your garden. Watch it fly around, and enjoy the flowers.

By observing the butterfly's life cycle, you'll learn about their different stages, from an egg to a caterpillar, then a chrysalis, and finally a butterfly.

How to Interact with Garden Wildlife

Interacting with garden wildlife is exciting, but if you're going to do it, you must do it right.

Bird Feeders

A bird feeder can help you interact with garden wildlife.[69]

1. Find a sturdy plastic bottle or an empty milk carton.
2. Ask an adult to help you cut a small hole near the bottom of the bottle or carton.
3. Decorate the bottle or carton with colorful paint or markers.
4. Punch two small holes near the top and thread a string through them to hang the feeder.
5. Fill the feeder with birdseed or small pieces of fruit.
6. Hang it in a tree or on a pole in your garden.
7. Watch from a distance and enjoy seeing different birds visit your feeder.

Bug Hotel

1. Get a small wooden box or container with a lid.
2. Decorate the box if you want to make it look pretty.
3. Make different levels and rooms inside the box using sticks, twigs, and branches.
4. Put pine cones, bamboo, or hollow reeds in some rooms for insects to hide and lay eggs.
5. Fill other rooms with dry leaves or straws to create spaces for insects to rest.
6. Find a quiet spot in your garden to place the tiny house.
7. Dig a shallow hole and partly bury the box, leaving the entrance accessible. Or use a string or wire to secure the box to a tree branch or stake.
8. Check the tiny house regularly and add new materials when needed.
9. Watch and learn about the insects that visit the tiny house.
10. Don't use any harmful chemicals in your garden to keep the insects safe.

Garden Games

Here are some fun garden-based games and activities you can enjoy with your family and friends.

Scavenger Hunt

1. Make a list of items that can be found in the garden, like a particular leaf, a flower, a rock, or a feather.
2. Give each player a copy of the list and a bag to collect their treasures.
3. Set a timer and see who can find all the items on the list first.

Nature Bingo

1. Create bingo cards with pictures of things you might find in the garden, such as a ladybug, a butterfly, a tree, or a bird.
2. Give each player a bingo card and a pen or marker.
3. Explore the garden together and mark off the items on your card as you spot them.

4. The first person to get a line or a full card marked off yells, "Bingo!" and wins the game.

Garden Obstacle Course
1. Set up a fun obstacle course in your garden using objects you find, like hula hoops, cones, or jump ropes.
2. Create challenges like hopping through hoops, zig-zagging between cones, or balancing on a log.
3. Time each player as they complete the course and see who can finish it the fastest.

Thank You Message

Thank you for choosing this book and taking an interest in gardening. Your efforts and enthusiasm in exploring the world of gardening are impressive. Seeing your love for nature blossoming and your skills and knowledge growing alongside it is amazing. Your curiosity and willingness to learn are enough to truly inspire everyone else around you!

As you went through this book, you discovered the pure magic behind watching a tiny seed transform into a beautiful flower or the healthiest vegetable. You've learned about the importance of sunshine, water, and soil for your plants. You've seen how gardening can light up your day and give you something to look forward to.

The garden is a place filled with endless possibilities. It's a means to connect with the natural world, care for plants, and create your own little piece of paradise. It is not just about growing pretty flowers or edible greens. It's a celebration of nature and all the amazing creatures that work together to keep the natural world alive. It is about taking care of the environment.

You'll be an amazing gardener! Always remember the positive and encouraging message this book carries. Don't stop being curious about the wonderful world of gardening. Nature is waiting for you to discover all her secrets through your love for plants and animals. Your skills and experience will grow just like the flowers in a garden because you can do incredible things. Believe in yourself, go out there, and let your green thumbs lead the way!

Here's another book by Dion Rosser that you might like

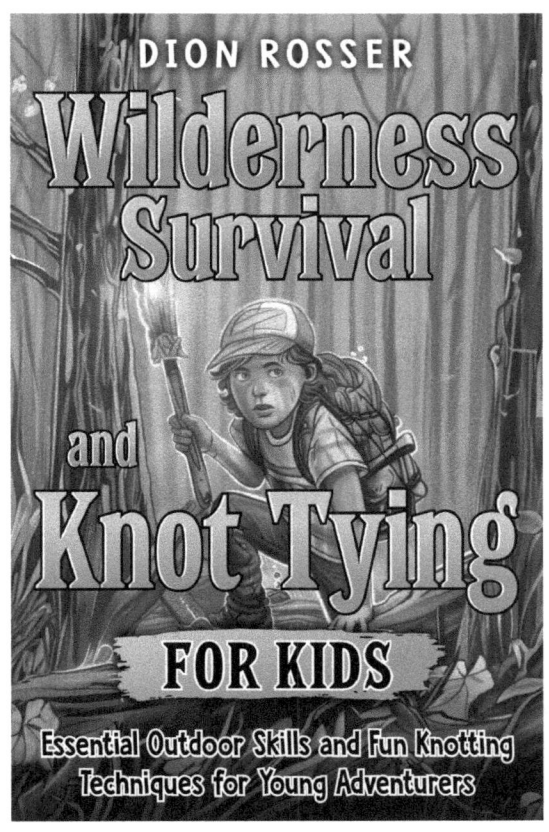

References

10 essential outdoor survival tips. (n.d.). Nuvancehealth.Org. https://www.nuvancehealth.org/health-tips-and-news/10-essential-outdoor-survival-tips

3 Things You MUST Teach Children for Wilderness Survival. (n.d.). Survivalfitnessplan.Com. https://www.survivalfitnessplan.com/blog/wilderness-survival-lessons-children

Basic Knots. (2019, January 11). Animatedknots.com. https://www.animatedknots.com/basic-knots

Biggers, S. (2019, October 19). The Adhesives and Glues Every Prepper Needs. Backdoor Survival. https://www.backdoorsurvival.com/the-adhesives-and-glues-every-prepper-needs/

Biggers, S. (2020, April 8). Survival Skills List: 75 Important Skills From Basic To Advanced. Backdoor Survival. https://www.backdoorsurvival.com/survival-skills/

Brown, T., & Morgan, A. B., Jr. (2023, April 4). Making cordage from natural materials. Mother Earth News – The Original Guide To Living Wisely; Mother Earth News. https://www.motherearthnews.com/diy/making-cordage-natural-materials-zmaz83jfzraw/

Bushcraft basics - the ultimate beginners' guide - HANWAG STORIES. (2023, March 31).

Chowdhury, M. R. (2023, October 13). The positive effects of nature on your mental wellbeing. PositivePsychology.com. https://positivepsychology.com/positive-effects-of-nature/

Dale, A. (n.d.). What are the Essential Wilderness Skills? Tech Writer EDC. https://techwriteredc.com/the-art-of-survival-mastering-the-essential-skills-for-thriving-in-the-wilderness/

Dedman, G. (2019, December 2). 12 Essential items people should have with them when they venture outdoors. Bushcraft Survival Australia. https://bushcraftsurvivalaustralia.com.au/12-essential-items-people-should-have-with-them-when-they-venture-outdoors/

Dedman, G. (2021, January 31). Cordage - something you should never be without. Bushcraft Survival Australia. https://bushcraftsurvivalaustralia.com.au/cordage-something-you-should-never-be-without/

Dedman, G. (2022, August 10). Water acquisition and purification. Bushcraft Survival Australia. https://bushcraftsurvivalaustralia.com.au/water-acquisition-and-purification/

DeRushie, N. (2020). Fire and cooking. Woodland Bushcraft. https://www.woodlandbushcraft.com/fireandcooking

End, S. A. (2022, January 22). How to build a survival shelter in the wild. Survive After End. https://surviveafterend.com/how-to-build-a-survival-shelter-in-the-wild/

Environment, & Climate Change. (n.d.). Trapping and harvesting - kids and teachers. Gov.Nt.Ca. https://www.gov.nt.ca/ecc/en/services/trapping-and-harvesting/trapping-and-harvesting-kids-and-teachers

Fire Craft 101. (n.d.). Slideshare.net. https://www.slideshare.net/kevinestela/fire-craft-101-presentation

Foraging for beginners: Tips for safely gathering wild, edible foods. Waterproof, Windproof & Breathable Clothing. (2017, November 8). https://www.gore-tex.com/blog/foraging-food-wild-plants

FutureLearn. (2023, June 9). The importance of first aid: 5 reasons to learn. FutureLearn. https://www.futurelearn.com/info/blog/the-importance-of-learning-first-aid-5-reasons-to-learn

FutureLearn. (2023, June 9). The importance of first aid: 5 reasons to learn. FutureLearn. https://www.futurelearn.com/info/blog/the-importance-of-learning-first-aid-5-reasons-to-learn

Gebhardt, M. (n.d.). Outdoor skills: Meaning, definition, origin. Survival Kompass. https://survival-kompass.de/dictionary/outdoor-skills/

Graham, S. (2023, May 5). How to Make Glue in the Wild: A Comprehensive Guide. Glue Savior. https://gluesavior.com/how-to-make-glue-in-the-wild/

Handling food safely while eating outdoors. (2022, February 17). U.S. Food and Drug Administration; FDA. https://www.fda.gov/food/buy-store-serve-safe-food/handling-food-safely-while-eating-outdoors

Harbour, S. (2020, December 15). Wilderness survival kits for kids: What to include? An Off Grid Life. https://www.anoffgridlife.com/wilderness-survival-kits-for-kids/

How to choose a wilderness campsite. (n.d.). Wilderness.net. https://wilderness.net/learn-about-wilderness/benefits/outdoor-recreation/camping/where-to-camp.php

How to tie a bowline knot. (n.d.). Rmg.co.uk. https://www.rmg.co.uk/stories/topics/how-tie-bowline-knot

Hurley, T. (2011, March 17). Outdoor cooking safety. LoveToKnow. https://www.lovetoknow.com/food-drink/meal-ideas/outdoor-cooking-safety

Hypothermia. (n.d.). WebMD. https://www.webmd.com/a-to-z-guides/what-is-hypothermia

James, J. (2020, March 17). 7 best ropes for survival based on uses and situation. Survival Freedom; Jim James. https://survivalfreedom.com/7-best-ropes-for-survival-based-on-uses-and-situation/

Leave no trace. (2023, September 6). The 7 principles - leave no trace center for outdoor ethics. Leave No Trace. https://lnt.org/why/7-principles/

Life, T. M. O. (2020, July 1). Nine natural shelters that can save your life in the wild. Popular Science. https://www.popsci.com/story/diy/natural-shelters-save-life-wild/

MacWelch, T. (2013, February 21). Survival skills: How to scout a good campsite. Outdoor Life. https://www.outdoorlife.com/blogs/survivalist/2013/02/survival-skills-how-scout-good-campsite/

MacWelch, T. (2020, October 12). How to process and use animal sinew. Outdoor Life. https://www.outdoorlife.com/story/survival/how-to-process-and-use-animal-sinew/

Nalanda. (2023, September 26). How to plan your first outdoor adventure as a family with kids. Medium. https://medium.com/digital-global-traveler/how-to-plan-your-first-outdoor-adventure-as-a-family-with-kids-1bbaa961eb70

Nesbitt, E. (2023, September 8). The benefits of teaching your kids bushcraft and survival skills. Wildlings Forest School. https://www.wildlingsforestschool.com/blog/bushcraft-and-survival-life-skills

Off The Grid. (2010, September 7). Staying warm in an emergency - Insulation. Off Grid Survival - Wilderness & Urban Survival Skills. https://offgridsurvival.com/emergencyinsulation/

Onbekend, T. (n.d.). Knowing survival firecraft can save your life. Extopian. https://extopian.com/outdoors/knowing-survival-fire-craft-can-save-your-life/

Owen, R. (2016, July 18). Camping in unfavorable weather: What to pack. The National Wildlife Federation Blog. https://blog.nwf.org/2016/06/camping-in-unfavorable-weather-what-to-pack/

Poffe, B. (2015, May 22). Bushcraft family, reconnect with nature. Rewilding Drum België; Rewilding Drum. https://www.rewildingdrum.be/bushcraft-good-for-your-tribe-good-for-you/

Rejba, A. (2019, July 1). Why is Shelter Needed for Survival? The Smart Survivalist Blog. https://www.thesmartsurvivalist.com/why-is-shelter-needed-for-survival/

Safety Kits Plus. (2021, May 21). First Aid Kits For Hiking & adventures. Safety Kits Plus. https://www.safetykitsplus.com/blogs/safety/first-aid-kits-for-hiking

Safety Kits Plus. (2021, May 21). First Aid Kits For Hiking & adventures. Safety Kits Plus. https://www.safetykitsplus.com/blogs/safety/first-aid-kits-for-hiking

Sherpa, S. (n.d.). Fire craft skills –. Survival Sherpa. https://survivalsherpa.wordpress.com/tag/fire-craft-skills/

Spera, J. (2018, May 8). Camping gear: 27 essentials for camping with kids. Today's Parent: SJC Media. https://www.todaysparent.com/family/activities/camping-gear-essentials-kids/

Spirit, B. (n.d.). Survival basics. Survival Basics | Bushcraft Spirit. https://www.bushcraftspirit.com/survival-basics/

Stricklin, T. (2023, October 5). 15 dangerous diseases caused by contaminated drinking water. SpringWell Water Filtration Systems. https://www.springwellwater.com/15-dangerous-diseases-caused-by-contaminated-drinking-water/

Survival hunting and trapping. (2015, September 14). Survival Skills and Bushcraft for the Modern Survivalist. https://yostsurvivalskills.com/survival-hunting-trapping/

Survival, A. (n.d.). Fire Craft. Armstrong Survival. https://armstrongsurvival.com/tag/fire-craft/

Tautline hitch. (n.d.). Netknots.com. https://www.netknots.com/rope_knots/tautline-hitch

Teaching basic first aid to kids. (2020, December 14). RUN WILD MY CHILD. https://runwildmychild.com/teaching-first-aid/

Teaching basic first aid to kids. (2020, December 14). RUN WILD MY CHILD. https://runwildmychild.com/teaching-first-aid/

Teaching CPR to children. (2019, March 15). HSI. https://hsi.com/solutions/cpr-aed-first-aid-training/resources-media/blog/teaching-cpr-to-children

Teaching CPR to children. (2019, March 15). HSI. https://hsi.com/solutions/cpr-aed-first-aid-training/resources-media/blog/teaching-cpr-to-children

What's the best material to use for waterproofing a survival shelter? (2019, January 12). Bushcraft Buddy. https://bushcraftbuddy.com/whats-the-best-material-to-use-for-waterproofing-a-survival-shelter/

Wilderness survival shelter. (n.d.). Bushcraftspirit.com. http://www.bushcraftspirit.com/wilderness-survival-shelter/

Wilderness survival: Fire & Knives. (n.d.). Trackerspdx.com. https://trackerspdx.com/youth/halloween-camps/wilderness-survival-fall-fire-knives.php

Wilderness Survival: Firecraft. (n.d.). Wilderness-survival.net. https://www.wilderness-survival.net/chp7.php

Wilderness survival. (n.d.). Mountainshepherd.com. https://mountainshepherd.com/home-2/wilderness-survival/

Williams, T. (2023, June 27). How to build a shelter: Your home away from home. Desert Island Survival. https://www.desertislandsurvival.com/how-to-build-a-shelter/

Willis, D. (n.d.). What is Bushcraft? Bushcraft with David Willis. http://www.davidwillis.info/what-is-bushcraft

Alsuwaidi, N. A. (2017, March 20). Little Gardener. Createspace Independent Publishing Platform.

Bone, E., & Wheatley, A. (2015, January 1). Gardening for Beginners.

Collins, C., & Lia, L. (2017, April 4). Grow Your Own for Kids. Mitchell Beazley.

Cutler, K. D., Fisher, K., DeJohn, S., & Association, N. G. (2010, October 29). Herb Gardening For Dummies. John Wiley & Sons.

Flint, M. L. (2018, January 1). Pests of the Garden and Small Farm, 3rd Edition. UCANR Publications.

Gaines, J. (2019, March 26). We Are the Gardeners. Thomas Nelson.

Gosling, L. (2023, February 28). My First Garden. DK Publishing (Dorling Kindersley).

Hogner, D. C. (1974, January 1). Good Bugs and Bad Bugs in Your Garden.

Krezel, C. (2010, April 1). Kids' Container Gardening. Chicago Review Press.

Lovejoy, S. (2017, January 24). Roots, Shoots, Buckets & Boots. Hachette UK.

Pierce, T. (2019, May 7). My Busy Green Garden.

Tai, L. (2021, March 15). The Magic of Children's Gardens. Temple University Press

Image Sources

[1] https://www.pexels.com/photo/family-standing-near-the-campfire-in-the-woods-9210491/

[2] https://www.pexels.com/photo/first-aid-kit-on-gray-background-5673523/

[3] https://www.pexels.com/photo/green-and-white-tents-near-trees-939723/

[4] https://www.pexels.com/photo/waterfall-seen-from-tent-15310519/

[5] Teejaybee, CC BY-NC-ND 2.0 DEED <https://creativecommons.org/licenses/by-nc-nd/2.0/> https://www.flickr.com/photos/teejaybee/8591215307

[6] Francois Boulogne, CC BY-SA 3.0 <https://creativecommons.org/licenses/by-sa/3.0>, via Wikimedia Commons
https://commons.wikimedia.org/wiki/File:Firesteel_light_my_fire_army_model.jpg

[7] https://www.peakpx.com/526025/blue-and-stainless-steel-thermal-carafe

[8] https://www.pexels.com/photo/person-holding-a-compass-3832684/

[9] https://www.wallpaperflare.com/man-standing-beside-camping-tent-wearing-headlamp-during-nighttime-man-using-headlamp-beside-cabin-tent-wallpaper-zmonu

[10] https://www.wallpaperflare.com/hiking-backpacks-on-grass-with-mountains-background-blue-and-red-camping-bag-on-green-grass-field-wallpaper-zhowh

[11] https://www.pexels.com/photo/children-in-winter-clothes-sitting-inside-a-tent-reading-books-6482318/

[12] https://www.pexels.com/photo/compass-placed-on-a-world-map-8828681/

[13] https://www.pexels.com/photo/first-aid-kit-on-gray-background-5673523/

[14] Joseph, CC BY-SA 2.0 DEED < https://creativecommons.org/licenses/by-sa/2.0/>
https://www.flickr.com/photos/umnak/14262748579

[15] https://www.pexels.com/photo/snow-on-rocky-mountain-peak-19168467/

[16] Ji-Elle, CC BY-SA 3.0 <https://creativecommons.org/licenses/by-sa/3.0>, via Wikimedia Commons: https://commons.wikimedia.org/wiki/File:Cordage_en_chanvre.jpg

[17] David J. Fred, CC BY-SA 2.5 <https://creativecommons.org/licenses/by-sa/2.5>, via Wikimedia Commons: https://commons.wikimedia.org/wiki/File:Paracord-Commercial-Type-III.jpg

[18] Angelsharum, CC BY-SA 3.0 <https://creativecommons.org/licenses/by-sa/3.0>, via Wikimedia Commons: https://commons.wikimedia.org/wiki/File:Nylon_Rope.JPG

[19] https://commons.wikimedia.org/wiki/File:Knot_square.jpg

[20] Buz11, CC BY-SA 4.0 <https://creativecommons.org/licenses/by-sa/4.0>, via Wikimedia Commons: https://commons.wikimedia.org/wiki/File:Bowline_tying.png

[21] David J. Fred, CC BY-SA 2.5 <https://creativecommons.org/licenses/by-sa/2.5>, via Wikimedia Commons: https://commons.wikimedia.org/wiki/File:TautlineHitch-ABOK-1800.jpg

[22] https://commons.wikimedia.org/wiki/File:EB1911_-_Knot_-_Fig._13_-_Clove_Hitch.jpg

[23] https://www.pickpik.com/tent-shelter-homeless-hut-cover-tarp-rectangular-117012

[24] GabeD, CC BY-NC-ND 2.0 DEED< https://creativecommons.org/licenses/by-nc-nd/2.0/> https://www.flickr.com/photos/augustuspics/7043841387

[25] https://www.wallpaperflare.com/photo-of-gray-cave-nature-landscape-shelter-hiding-place-wallpaper-wffwt

[26] https://commons.wikimedia.org/wiki/File:Field-expedient_lean-to_and_fire_reflector.jpg

[27] Jomegat, CC BY-SA 3.0 <https://creativecommons.org/licenses/by-sa/3.0>, via Wikimedia Commons: https://commons.wikimedia.org/wiki/File:Pole_tarp_and_rope_shelter_4855.JPG

[28] Photo by Dajana Reçi https://www.pexels.com/photo/bonfire-on-desert-at-dusk-16386940/

[29] https://www.wallpaperflare.com/burning-wood-surrounded-with-snow-camp-fire-winter-outdoor-wallpaper-whkdx

[30] https://www.pexels.com/photo/abstract-beach-bright-clouds-301599/

[31] Dave Gough, CC BY 2.0 DEED <https://creativecommons.org/licenses/by/2.0/> https://www.flickr.com/photos/spacepleb/1505372433

[32] https://www.pickpik.com/fire-camping-camp-nature-campfire-forest-91264

[33] https://pixabay.com/vectors/campfire-wood-fire-firewood-31930/

[34] https://commons.wikimedia.org/wiki/File:Methods_of_laying_fires.jpg

[35] https://pixabay.com/vectors/water-drink-body-human-hydration-5767178/

[36] SMART Servier Medical Art, CC BY-SA 3.0 <https://creativecommons.org/licenses/by-sa/3.0>, via Wikimedia Commons: https://commons.wikimedia.org/wiki/File:Boiling_water_in_a_pan.png

[37] Sankar 1995, CC BY-SA 4.0 <https://creativecommons.org/licenses/by-sa/4.0>, via Wikimedia Commons: https://commons.wikimedia.org/wiki/File:Orange_Nasturtium_Flower_-_Shola_Gardens_-_Kotagiri.jpg

[38] Zeynel Cebeci, CC BY-SA 4.0 <https://creativecommons.org/licenses/by-sa/4.0>, via Wikimedia Commons: https://commons.wikimedia.org/wiki/File:Taraxacum_officinale_-_Common_dandelion_03.jpg

³⁹ Rizka, CC BY-SA 4.0 <https://creativecommons.org/licenses/by-sa/4.0>, via Wikimedia Commons: https://commons.wikimedia.org/wiki/File:Doll%27s_Eyes,_Mount_Auburn_Cemetery,_Cambridge,_Massachusetts.jpg

⁴⁰ Alvesgaspar, CC BY-SA 3.0 <http://creativecommons.org/licenses/by-sa/3.0/>, via Wikimedia Commons: https://commons.wikimedia.org/wiki/File:Nerium_oleander_flowers_leaves.jpg

⁴¹ Jason Pratt from Pittsburgh, PA, CC BY 2.0 <https://creativecommons.org/licenses/by/2.0>, via Wikimedia Commons: https://commons.wikimedia.org/wiki/File:Cooking_Hot_Dogs_on_the_Campfire_(3677843356).jpg

⁴² https://pixabay.com/vectors/questions-man-head-success-lamp-2519654/

⁴³ https://pixabay.com/vectors/band-aid-first-aid-medical-adhesive-3116999/

⁴⁴ © Raimond Spekking: CC BY-SA 4.0 DEED <https://creativecommons.org/licenses/by-sa/4.0/deed> https://commons.wikimedia.org/wiki/File:Pr%C3%A4meta_tourniquet-4981.jpg

⁴⁵ https://commons.wikimedia.org/wiki/File:Cardiopulmonary_Resuscitation_Adult.jpg

⁴⁶ https://www.pexels.com/photo/person-fishing-294674/

⁴⁷ https://pixabay.com/vectors/paw-print-paw-foot-prints-footprint-2165814/

⁴⁸ https://commons.wikimedia.org/wiki/File:Distress_Signals.png

⁴⁹ https://www.pexels.com/photo/green-grass-field-13975/

⁵⁰ https://www.pexels.com/photo/assorted-color-flowers-298246/

⁵¹ https://www.pexels.com/photo/person-watering-a-potted-plant-4503268/

⁵² https://www.pexels.com/photo/person-wearing-green-gloves-holding-garden-tools-7782975/

⁵³ WayneRay, CC BY-SA 4.0 <https://creativecommons.org/licenses/by-sa/4.0>, via Wikimedia Commons: https://commons.wikimedia.org/wiki/File:Watering_can_WPC6.JPG

⁵⁴ https://www.pexels.com/photo/person-digging-on-soil-using-garden-shovel-1301856/

⁵⁵ Photo by Joanna Kosinska on Unsplash https://unsplash.com/photos/blueberries-on-white-ceramic-container-4qujjbj3srs

⁵⁶ Photo by Marius Ciocirlan on Unsplash https://unsplash.com/photos/orange-pumpkins-on-gray-field-near-green-grassland-at-daytime-selective-focus-photography-T9pdHqCsyoQ

⁵⁷ Photo by Yakov Leonov on Unsplash https://unsplash.com/photos/green-leaves-in-macro-lens-0wWYos3ZGqU

⁵⁸ Photo by Julia Kwiek on Unsplash https://unsplash.com/photos/orange-flowers-with-green-leaves-2j8X-RpB1sM

⁵⁹ https://unsplash.com/photos/purple-and-yellow-flower-in-tilt-shift-lens-Md_rDAJxRLM?utm_content=creditShareLink&utm_medium=referral&utm_source=unsplash

⁶⁰ https://www.pexels.com/photo/vegetables-harvest-fresh-basket-175414/

⁶¹ https://commons.wikimedia.org/wiki/File:Wild_strawberries_ARS.jpg

⁶² https://unsplash.com/photos/honeybee-perching-on-yellow-flower-yxXpjF-RrnA?utm_content=creditShareLink&utm_medium=referral&utm_source=unsplash

[63] https://unsplash.com/photos/macro-photography-of-orange-and-black-bug-perching-on-plant-906sxg0humM?utm_content=creditShareLink&utm_medium=referral&utm_source=unsplash

[64] Photo by Ingo Doerrie on Unsplash https://unsplash.com/photos/close-up-photography-of-beetle-btmrHN8V3B0

[65] xpda, CC BY-SA 4.0 <https://creativecommons.org/licenses/by-sa/4.0>, via Wikimedia Commons: https://commons.wikimedia.org/wiki/File:Aleyrodidae_P1560540a.jpg

[66] Sharon Mollerus, CC BY 2.0 <https://creativecommons.org/licenses/by/2.0>, via Wikimedia Commons: https://commons.wikimedia.org/wiki/File:Field_of_Weeds_(2636333676).jpg

[67] Photo by Roman Synkevych on Unsplash https://unsplash.com/photos/green-plant-sprouting-at-daytime-fjj7lVpCxRE

[68] Sri2161k, CC BY-SA 4.0 <https://creativecommons.org/licenses/by-sa/4.0>, via Wikimedia Commons: https://commons.wikimedia.org/wiki/File:Pebbles_6.jpg

[69] https://unsplash.com/photos/brown-bird-on-red-wooden-bird-house-vkDh08uoNJg?utm_content=creditShareLink&utm_medium=referral&utm_source=unsplash

www.ingramcontent.com/pod-product-compliance
Lightning Source LLC
Chambersburg PA
CBHW051851160426
43209CB00006B/1257